THE
STUDENT
JOURNALIST
GUIDE
SERIES

THE STUDENT JOURNALIST AND THE
NEWSMAGAZINE FORMAT

by
ELAINE H. PRITCHETT

PUBLISHED BY
Richards Rosen
Press, Inc.
New York

Published in 1976 by Richards Rosen Press, Inc.
29 East 21st Street, New York, N.Y. 10010

Copyright 1976 by Elaine H. Pritchett

All rights reserved. No part of this book may be reproduced
in any form without written permission from
the publisher, except by a reviewer.

First Edition

Library of Congress Cataloging in Publication Data

Pritchett, Elaine H
 The student journalist and the newsmagazine format.

 (The student journalist guide series)
 Bibliography: p.
 1. College and school journalism. I. Title.
LB3621.P74   371.8'97   75-35664
ISBN 0-8239-0340-0

Manufactured in the United States of America

*The Student Journalist
and the
NEWSMAGAZINE
FORMAT*

To Henry, the Papason to hundreds of adoring and adorable student staffers, the "second self" every journalism teacher needs to accomplish the task, and the one without whom many of our projects could not have been completed.

ABOUT THE AUTHOR

ELAINE H. PRITCHETT came to the teaching of journalism as the culmination of a career that had encompassed virtually every aspect of the field—editorial, promotional, advertising, and mechanical. Posts she has held include reporter, copywriter, photolithographer, promotion and publicity director, and editor. She has been Director of Journalism for the Spring Branch Independent School District in Houston, Texas, since 1961, except for intervals spent as instructor in journalism at Arizona State University and the Universities of Oklahoma and Iowa. She has also conducted Faculty-High School Press workshops in numerous states.

The school publications, both newspapers and yearbooks, put out under her advisership have been consistent award winners from such organizations as the Texas High School Press Association, the Columbia University Scholastic Press Association, the Quill and Scroll Society, and the National Scholastic Press Association.

Mrs. Pritchett's professional affiliations include membership in Theta Sigma Phil, Sigma Delta Chi, the Texas Association of Journalism Directors, the Columbia Scholastic Press Advisers Association, and others. She has been editor of The Forum section of *Communication: Journalism Education Today,* and has published articles in various professional journals.

Among personal honors accorded Mrs. Pritchett have been a Headliner award for outstanding achievement in communications from Theta Sigma Phi, a Gold Key for outstanding achievement in journalism education from the Columbia Scholastic Press Association, and the Teacher of the Year award of the Newspaper Fund.

Mrs. Pritchett is the holder of a B.S. degree in Journalism from Southern Methodist University and an M.A. degree in Journalism Education from Arizona State University.

ACKNOWLEDGMENTS

Special thanks are due a number of co-workers and many former students who have contributed to the evolution of this publication format. Among those exerting special influence or contributing directly to this volume are Chet Hunt, adviser to *The Bugle Call* at Robert E. Lee High School in San Antonio, Texas; Ben Van Zante, adviser to the *West Side Story,* West High School, Iowa City, Iowa; Randy Stano, *The Shield,* McCallum High School, Austin, Texas; Freeman Hover, *The Rincon Echo,* Rincon High School, Tucson, Arizona; Mrs. Betty Stanley, *The Monterey Mirror,* Monterey High School, Lubbock, Texas; Charles Rogers, *El Gato,* Westchester High School, and Mrs. Judy Sanders of Memorial High School's *The Anvil,* both in the Spring Branch School District, Houston, Texas; James Bouchay, *The Cadet Call,* Marmion Military Academy, Aurora, Illinois; Mrs. Terry Alexandris, *The Hobachi,* Redlands (California) High School; John Kulish, *The Torch,* John F. Kennedy High School, Bloomington, Minnesota; Fred Barry, Industrial Printing Co., Randy Elliott, Type-Rite Graphics Printing Co., and D-Eon Priest, Taylor Publishing Co., all of Houston, Texas.

For encouragement and professional inspiration, gratitude is extended to James F. Paschal of The University of Oklahoma. And, for accepting experimentation in the process of growth for *The Anvil* and its youthful staff members during my tenure at Spring Branch Memorial High School, Principal Wayne F. Schaper commands the deep love and respect of one who has been accorded trust and confidence.

E.H.P.

CONTENTS

      Introduction

I. *Basic Principles:* Understanding newsmagazine concepts • Meeting the information needs of the school readers • Organizing the staff and its activities.   19

II. *Visual Impact:* Using the excitement and convenience of magazine format to attract and hold readers • Establishing characteristics and variations of the format • Establishing the basic design • Choosing a printer • Setting the budget.   31

III. *Graphics Design:* Designing pages • Using type for readability and for communication of mood or tone • Applying the typographical schedule • Counting copy • Writing headlines • Employing special-design type faces • Dummying the pages.   45

IV. *Photographic Illustrations:* Striving for technical excellence • Cropping for better composition • Scaling for reproduction • Adding special effects • Using photos to convey the story • Writing cutlines.   87

V. *The All-Important Content:* Departmentalizing the content • Apportioning coverage • Finding story subjects • Writing specialized copy • Creating headlines.   99

VI. *Quality Control:* Observing format specifications • Making copy correct and compelling • Editing for style and comprehension • Keeping the visual image sharp • Avoiding unnecessary mistakes. 119

VII. *Special Techniques and Equipment:* Some ways to improve the finished product and cut costs at the printer's • Unusual typography • Printer-produced special effects • Patterned screens and darkroom tricks for photographs • Preprinted materials • Supplies and tools to achieve better results. 131

Appendices
   A. *Glossary* 145
   B. *Bibliography* 151

INTRODUCTION

The school news publication cannot truly duplicate the professional example so often used in the classroom, the metropolitan daily paper, in frequency of publication, size or number of pages, or even in philosophy, since it has a different relationship to its "government" than that of the free-enterprise public press. True, some functions of school publications are coincident with those of newspapers. So are some functions the same as for newsmagazines, for house organs, and for general or special-interest magazines. But school news publications need not be bound by rules that call for them to duplicate any single example.

School communication is a unique area of journalism. Some school publication staffs feel that they can better meet their responsibilities to their special publics by creating for themselves a unique format.

In the 1960's a few schools broke with the traditional miniature newspaper format, and a number of others have followed in their wake, quite often improving on the product. Innovation has been the key word in this trend toward a separate format for the school press. Some have used traditional print-media standards for their skeletal structure, building from there a more exciting and appealing publication. Others have been influenced by the so-called underground press, antiestablishment publications that emerged in the 1960's and proffered no allegiance to traditions of print communication. In this second decade of the search for a more relevant medium for the school press, the better efforts reflect the best of both of these plus workable ideas from all areas of the magazine industry.

The Student Journalist and the Newsmagazine Format

Weekly newsmagazines, Sunday supplements to the metropolitan dailies, special-interest periodicals, and the compelling graphics design in advertising are all influencing content and appearance of school publications in the 1970's. Students want something different of their "paper." They want information about subjects that concern them; they want more facts about news items than those they already know; they want interesting and amusing reading material. Above all, they demand visual appeal in anything they read. This generation is so photo-oriented that they expect excitement of design and turn away from anything that looks "dull."

It has become an accepted premise that school publications, removed as they are by philosophical differences from the professional press, need not be restricted to emulation of the physical aspects of newspaper giants they cannot hope to duplicate. There is recognition now that the school press is not a mere learning exercise, but is indeed an integral part of the school scene and an entity in itself. As a unique segment of the communications world, it is entitled to certain separate characteristics of content and appearance. The scholastic press associations have added the "newsmagazine" category to their critical review services for this group of "different" publications. Score books have been revised to include separate standards for assessing publications in this category because both physical and philosophical tenets in the newspaper rule books did not always apply. The new category was dubbed "newsmagazine" because the kind of content and style of makeup more closely followed those of the professional weekly magazines.

When a new product appears on the market, prospective consumers want a complete explanation of what it will do for them, how it is constructed, what makes it work, and how much it will cost. They ask for a detailed and concrete definition in understandable language.

While the newsmagazine is not an unfamiliar object, its adaptation to the school press is relatively new, and the term does have different connotations in this context. This effort is in response to the many times eager young journalists have asked, after seeing copies of school newsmagazines, "We'd like to try this. . . . Where can we get a book about it?"

The intent in this volume is to set forth some guidelines for prospective users of the format. Since there is no international authority on the school news publication, each staff is free to create its own structure and to adapt to its own use whatever is applicable. Anyone is entitled to write new rules or a whole new game. The "rules" set forth herein are offered in the effort to provide workable guidelines coupled with good journalistic standards. The staffs employing them are urged to weigh both agreements and disagreements with the text in light of their own school situation. As each institution reflects to some extent the philosophy and attitude of its administration, so will its publication. There is no set of rules for guiding all institutions of learning; there can be no absolute rules for all school publications. Readers are invited to use what fits their situation, condemn what they disagree with, argue over what puzzles them. The author requests, simply, that the effort be accepted as a sincere attempt to pass along an eclectic overview of good newsmagazine journalism for the school press.

*The Student Journalist
and the
NEWSMAGAZINE
FORMAT*

Chapter I

BASIC PRINCIPLES

The functions of the school news publication have shifted in recent years to extend beyond the recording of campus activities. The broadening of student interests has called for an expansion of coverage in the school paper. The increased sophistication of the teen-ager has demanded a higher level of approach to the content, better writing, and a more dynamic appearance.

Many student staffs are finding that they can better meet the demands of their readers, and better compete for readers, through use of the newsmagazine format. The term newsmagazine is used for lack of a more definitive term; it does not imply that the school publication can be a copy of the professional weekly, just as it cannot possibly duplicate the metropolitan daily paper. There is more probability, however, of adapting magazine journalism to the school publication.

Proponents of the format find it two ways better: a more appealing appearance and a more satisfying approach with copy. The publication looks more inviting to the youthful audience because of exciting graphics, more alive-looking pages. There is visual appeal through an integration of illustrations, display type, body copy, and white space with what is called graphics design. Artistic arrangement of these elements works to form a visual expression of the mood or tone of a piece. This kind of display serves first to interest the reader, then carries a pleasant feeling through for double impact.

Like the speaker who establishes rapport with the audience at the outset by telling jokes and timely stories, so the school publication can enhance its reader appeal with the excitement of a classy giftwrap appearance. Today's visually oriented television generation responds favorably to attractive design.

Naturally, if a gift package is all wrap and no content, it will soon be discarded as an empty box. That is why content is of equal importance to design. It is through the different approach to content that the newsmagazine sustains appeal for the reluctant-to-read student population.

Magazine Copy

Newsmagazine approach to copy can provide more interesting material. Since school publications seldom can tell the news first within their publication schedule, they must tell it better. A good newsmagazine will give information the readers do not have, but want or need to know. Information that can be made use of *now* is what the student reader appreciates, rather than just a documentation of known facts for personal recognition or the permanent record, important as these writings may be.

Content and copy approach differ within the newsmagazine category according to the aim or purpose of each publication. Some magazines strive to have something for everyone in every issue. Others with an editorial emphasis concentrate on "guarding the reader's rights" and "watchdogging" situations that might work against the readers' best interests (as seen from that staff's point of view). Still others try to strike a medium between these in an effort to reach the majority of potential readers at some time through the publication's annum. They offer a variety of content with a measure of crusading, yet serve the basic functions still required of a school news publication: to inform, to educate, and to entertain. Then there are those purely feature magazines containing a majority of articles in areas of student interest and entertainment. When no space is given to news items, however, these magazines should be supplemented with in-school mimeographed or duplicated papers, or with frequent newscasts on the public-address system or closed-circuit television. Even a bulletin board would be better than no news reporting at all. For purposes of the permanent record, it remains the responsibility of the student press to record school events and reflect practices and attitudes of the times. No one else is keeping score on details of the whole picture.

News Treatment

In the newsmagazine format, news is not ignored, but each item receives treatment commensurate with its relative importance to the entire school. Less important news items are tightly written, condensed, and recorded in a "news briefs" column or noted in the calendar of coming events. This requires careful, accurate writing to get the important facts in the smallest space. And it allows room for treating major news events in depth with more concentration on the why and the how elements. That higher level of approach to content calls for depth reporting, interpretive articles, news analysis, explanatory and background features, action accounts, and personality profiles. Diminutive newspaper-style makeup is not so well suited to use of such longer articles.

With the purposes of informing, educating, and entertaining, then, the school newsmagazine serves four functions of current and lasting value to its institution: (1) to record school events and the activities of persons who make up the school community; (2) to report on the meaning and significance of major events or situations for purposes of edification; (3) to review signs of the times and capture for present and future readers the attitudes and reactions of the school population to significant events—capture more than the facts on record, reflect the fads and fashions of the times; and (4) to relate to the readers with content of interest to that particular audience which no other publication can reach so well. Establishing this last important reason for being, the school publication that has rapport with its readers will achieve the credibility needed to exert leadership, and, thereby, can be of greater service to all through better serving the individuals.

The newsmagazine format allows the staff more readily to achieve these functions in content because it fosters emphasis on the areas that have greater impact on the reader. By condensing less important news items or briefs or the calendar, more space is made available for an investigative look at the real issues of the day. Devoting a whole page to one article permits use of several accompanying photos or a large drawing to help carry the message. Big news stories are reported, not just recorded. Background information, the relationship of one set of facts to other situations, and the significance of the information can be pointed out. How or why something occurred or what it means in terms of the immediate future are questions the reader wants and needs to have answered. It takes enterprise, a strong measure of responsibility, and a good show of maturity for a student reporter to glean the information necessary for such accounting, and to give an honest reporting. It requires more than a few column inches of copy to give a full account of complex news events, especially if there is conflicting opinion already in the arena.

Of course, not all major news events are controversial in nature. Some big news stories, such as school drama productions or the appearance of celebrities on campus, probably will be treated as news features. Some accounts will take on an eyewitness flair, or reporters may become involved to the point of writing from a participant's angle. These kinds of stories all have greater reader appeal than surface fact accounts; they involve the reader in the story. Names of participants need not be omitted. Names do make news. Yet the reader wants to know not only of the cast and crew, but also about the trials encountered by the prop committee and the problems that beset the scenery builders. Humanizing the news accounts enhances their interest for the reader and sharpens the portrayal of a routine news event recorded for posterity. In magazine format, the required space can be allotted, even to including several pictures for added impact.

Magazine-type articles on current interests and activities come under the heading of education or entertainment. They offer information readers can use directly (such as understanding some new pursuit, knowing where to go or what there is to do, learning how to make something), or they provide moments of entertainment for reader relaxation (an indirect but very useful function.)

Reader Involvement

Perhaps one of the most popular features is the forum for exchange of ideas and opinions among readers. A really functioning letters-to-the-editor column can increase and sustain reader interest through participation. Strong editorials on important subjects, with an open invitation for feedback, will sometimes bring in letters. Guest editorials or a signed editor's column may do the same. An ombudsman (or ombudsperson) column may be added to attract reader participation. In such a column, a staff member receives questions from readers and then interviews authoritative sources. Reader involvement can be injected through opinion polls and surveys, or through symposium-type interviews. Symposium interviews should be held among persons with appropriate background to offer significant responses, and their authoritative status established. Polls of an informal nature might be conducted for short reactions to a current event to get names of readers in print as well as to capture current attitudes. The editorial staff should work at making reader reaction important; content must be meaty if any reaction is to be expected. No controversy, no substance, then nothing is there to warrant a reply.

People like to read about themselves and about people they know. They like to see pictures of their friends, and a people-oriented department will be a popular section if well handled—not the old "student of the month" spotlight on the likes and pet peeves of already prominent persons on campus. Good people-oriented copy deals with unusual accomplishments or interests and with the philosophy and motivations of individuals, such as the principal who rides in rodeos on weekends or the freshman girl gymnast training for the Olympics. Everyone has an interesting story to relate if an enterprising, inquiring reporter will just ferret it out.

Dividing Content: Uniting Staff

Characteristic of the newsmagazine format is departmentalization of content—grouping articles of like nature into adjacent pages or columns. All news, sports, opinion, features, and special-interest articles are grouped for subject emphasis and so labeled. The reader then knows where to find favorite segments. Departmentalizing the content and displaying it in the same general sequence in each issue helps make the reader comfortable with a publication.

However, departmentalization is not only for reader convenience. It is a great help to the staff. Planning far ahead for long-range stories allows the staff time to research and rewrite for better quality. Quite logically, staff positions are assigned by "departments" rather than by pages. Such specialization places writers in areas of expertise. Feature writers should be working continuously on stories for specifically timed presentation and, all the while, storing a backlog of timeless articles that can be used when space permits or demands. Sportswriters are not only reporting the current season, they are compiling season statistics as they go and collecting features on individual athletic activities and recreational pursuits.

Yet, the entire staff must work closely together and preplan each issue in minute detail if the quality is to be consistently high. Departmentalization encourages assignment of staffers to take full advantage of their special talents, but it takes teamwork and flexibility to produce a top-notch edition every time. Titles and staff assignments should not serve divisive but cohesive purposes. Everyone does a bit of anything at deadline time.

As a group, the newsmagazine staff should discuss each issue well in advance of publication, planning content, special layout designs, cover, and editorial stands. If the editor is expected to "think of something" to write an editorial about at the last minute, the staff is missing the opportunity to make a significant contribution to its community. The staff is failing to meet its responsibilities of being the medium of influence it should be. An editorial page must be preplanned for maximum display effect and for content impact because a dull-looking page will probably go unread, and a weakly written editorial will likely go unheeded.

Editorial Board

Achieving an effective publication involves not only meetings of the entire staff before each issue, but also an editorial board conference of top editors preceding the staff discussion. The editorial board of three to five members should prepare a full plan for each issue with a view of the long-range picture. Persons worthy of top editorial positions should be able to formulate a complete assignment sheet and maintain a constant flow of good material to keep every issue filled with quality writing. Feedback and input from the entire staff are important and valuable. Reporters and photographers need to realize their importance to the effectiveness of each issue. Editors need to hear other ideas and suggestions to broaden the scope and to strengthen the impact of the publication. Staff meetings without structure, however, will take longer and be less effective than those based on specific areas of consideration. Too much diversity of input can consume too much time and create confusion.

PUBLICATIONS BOARD

Beyond staff meetings and editorial board conferences, many staffs find a publications board a valuable asset. Publications board members include persons outside the journalism component. Several faculty members who are liked and respected by the students, some students who represent a variety of interests (not just the Student Council president and class officers), even an open-minded administrator or two could be invited to meet with the editors and adviser several times a year for the purpose of assessing the value of the publication to its community. The value to the staff of meetings of the publications board is the acquisition of input on ways to increase effectiveness of the publication and on the merits of previous content. Since magazine journalism deals with a quantity of subjective material, some periodic appraisal of the course reading is important. It is a good idea to ask twice as many persons as needed, say, six teachers, ten to twelve students, and three or four counselors and principals. There will never be a time when all can be assembled at once. Busy schedules will cut attendance to half or less, no matter what day or time is set for meeting. Football players are not available in the fall, but might be able to participate in the spring when baseball or track personnel are busiest. Making social occasions of the meetings, serving soft drinks and cookies, and holding the gatherings in the staff office will add interest for the board members and will serve to establish a friendly atmosphere for congenial exchange of ideas.

GUIDELINES

Before setting about publishing a newsmagazine, the editorial board should establish policy guidelines that specifically stipulate the purpose of the publication, its aims and intents, its standards, and the rules under which it means to operate. This requires decisions on the handling of certain areas of content, language, and attitude. In preparing a publication's policy, the staff should have full knowledge of the Canons of Journalism adopted by the American Society of Newspaper Editors in 1927, which provides a sound basis for discussion of social responsibilities of the press. The Journalist's Creed, written by Walter Williams when he was Dean of the School of Journalism at The University of Missouri, is another document that sets forth desirable standards for journalistic endeavors. Most professional newspapers and newsmagazines hold the tenets in both as ideal standards. Most important, however, is that the staff members know where they stand and discuss among themselves what principles they hold desirable and what goals they have for the publication during their tenure. It is wise to set a policy on whether to require publishing of names with letters to the editor, for example. Although some circumstances might offer good argument for withholding names on request, what is to prevent authorities or opposing parties from claiming that the letters are not unsolicited comments, but are actually staff opinion under the guise of anonymity? Is the use of "street language" in print worth the loss of dignity it costs a publication? And what responsibilities accompany freedom of the press?

Of some import might be the kind of publication the staffs consider theirs to be: sounding board or bulletin board? crusader or documenter? reflector or image setter? There is no reason a newsmagazine cannot be all these, and more. It remains for the staffs to determine whose interests they will serve first, why they have accepted the job of putting out a publication on a continuing schedule, what they consider their basic function and subsequent functions, and where they stand on the special aims and purposes of their publications.

PUBLICATION POLICY POINTS

Points to ponder in formulating a publication's policy include: (*1*) the responsibilities to the entire school community as opposed to special-interest groups; (*2*) the call for accuracy and full information; (3) the call for objectivity in examination; (4) the need for specific guidelines on language usage, personal opinion expressions, and kinds of topics and issues to be discussed or avoided; and (5) an open commitment on where the editorial board stands in its relationship with school authorities, student readers, and the collective school community.

Once a solid policy has been adopted by the editorial board, it should be discussed with the school administration (principal and/or school board) from which any interference or opposition might arise. If a standard of operations can be agreed upon at the outset, there is likely to be more cooperation and less mistrust on all sides. Student journalists who exhibit maturity in approach will likely meet with less reproach and more open cooperation.

The chances for freedom to operate independently are greater for the student journalists who show intentions to perform responsibly, with mature judgment. When these intentions are verbalized in a clear-cut editorial policy, they should serve to alleviate apprehensions that many administrators have toward student publications. Generally these apprehensions stem from uncertainty about what the paper may do to upset whatever tranquillity exists. The editors and advisers who can dissolve these fears will serve their own purposes as well, because they not only are spared the constant vigilance of "authority" but also have an established course of action to follow.

No policy statement can encompass all possible problem areas, but the exercise of thinking through all the possibilities that come to mind will set a precedent for individual situations as they arise. Moreover, a written statement is a valuable ally in dealing with persons whose contributions might violate the good relations established with authorities and readers.

Duty Designations

Another written document that aids the student staff is a job manual. For effective preplanning, a publication needs a people structure wherein all participants understand their jobs and function with zeal and dedication. The job manual should explain the chain of authority and the specific duties of each area. Job descriptions should include duties, time elements, and follow-up activities—all responsibilities pertaining to each staff position, from editor-in-chief through advertising sales people. Do not overlook photography staffers, business department, exchange editors, and all writers, in addition to editorial positions. If editors and adviser feel it expedient, grounds for dismissal may be stated to avoid unpleasant or complicated situations that might arise if any person failed to perform accepted responsibilities.

Format Specifications

Also needed is a physical structure plan delineating the appearance of the publication. Such a structural plan includes all details of the format, a complete headline schedule, and type specifications for all elements in the basic plan. It also includes provisions for white space—margins, gutters, column widths, etc. All type sizes and faces for headings and copy are listed, their uses defined and explained, and the count per column or per pica noted. Rules for headlines, subheads, story breakers, by-lines, photo captions, photo credits, folios, and body copy variations are set forth so that all personnel can follow the same procedures. Consistency in physical appearance, particularly in small areas of type usage, marks a professional publication. If the rules are printed for each staff member, there should be no problem in maintaining consistency. Also helpful is a large poster on the wall of the journalism lab showing headline schedule and type specs.

Definition of the specific format is a significant step. The varieties and options open to publications in the newsmagazine category are discussed in Chapter II. Once the staff has settled on its format, contracted with a printer, laid down its rules and guidelines for operation, and organized the personnel, it is ready to embark on the exciting business of communicating.

In summary, the formula for a successful newsmagazine calls for:

1. Having an editorial board that functions: plans far in advance, understands its own goals, accepts its responsibilities, and meets with the staff to discuss each issue.
2. Having a publications board to give added dimension to the content and philosophy of the publication.

3. Having a clear-cut staff manual that all members understand.
4. Having a tight format that all staffers know and observe—margins, folio, type specs, basic design pattern, departmentalization and its sequence.
5. Having a stated set of principles and guidelines for content.
6. Having a definite set of goals for the year in editorial accomplishments.
7. Knowing the audience and remembering who is to be served by the publication's content.
8. Having a built-in flexibility: a backlog of good copy ready (and more working), a current oversupply of good art (photo features or cartoons that stand alone), an imaginative grasp of makeup and design, and a creative file of ideas for copy, cover designs, page layouts, and photographs.

Chapter II

VISUAL IMPACT

The visual dynamics of magazine format attracts the school audience and establishes an atmosphere of contemporary approach. The philosophy of the editorial content may well be reflected in the visual elements. Certainly it behooves a dignified publication to present the appearance of dignity in its format. A lively content deserves an exciting display. The reader is entitled to expect congruity in appearance and tone of content. And a classy look in a publication starts the reader off with a feeling of anticipation for good things to come. The popularity of the newsmagazine format has resulted in large measure from the initial appeal of exciting cover designs and interesting display of major content.

The basic differences in appearance that characterize the newsmagazine and the newspaper involve the use of space.

SPACE ALLOTMENT

Since the front page makes the initial impression, the use of dramatic cover designs is a strong weapon for the magazine. This means giving all of page 1 to photographs or drawings that will attract attention and lure the reader to inside content. Such use of page 1 is looked upon by magazine enthusiasts as advertising the content and as space well spent on reader appeal. The excitement of page design that attracts the student reader involves creative use of white space to frame the layout and direct the eye through large heading type and illustrations to copy. Departmentalization of content not only is advantageous to reader and staff, but also offers another area to add visual attractiveness to the pages. Plans for page design often include some dramatic way to identify the content classification on each spread. This involves use of wider margins or transfer of several lines of type in outside columns to space for such identifications.

Applying newsmagazine format to the school publication means thinking in terms of 12 to 20 pages per issue. Economy dictates multiples of four pages because most sheets make at least two pages on each run through the press. Larger presses print four or eight pages on each side of a sheet. A four-page school paper, though divided into news, opinion, feature, and sports pages, does not permit magazine makeup nor allow for longer articles in sufficient number to meet the qualifications for newsmagazine classification. The four-page, 11½ by 17-inch newspaper can be folded to make eight smaller pages. This increases the number of pages available for advertising and permits some use of dramatic display on the cover and center spread. It is certainly a step in the direction of visual appeal and will add excitement for those publications whose budgets do not permit use of more paper. It takes considerable skill in both writing and design to fulfill the functions of a school news publication in newsmagazine format with only eight pages, but it can be done.

One way to increase the number of pages might be to extend the time between issues and double the number of pages for each issue. Many school publications are distributed every three weeks or monthly. When the time between publication is stretched this far, it is even more important to write past news items more concisely, to concentrate on future events and ongoing stories, and to offer in-depth reports on situations that concern the readers. It is this kind of content that lends itself best to newsmagazine format.

Format Basics

The page size, kind of paper, basic type usage, and arrangement of content are key factors in the format of a publication. To begin, a staff must first draw up a set of constant physical characteristics—page size; structural patterns for margins, borders, column widths, copy, advertising, and departmentalization; and designs for standing column titles and treatment, departmental designators, and folio appearance and placement. Most publications are arranged on a vertical plan, higher than wide, and the width is always cited first in stating measurements, as 9 x 12. When a horizontal design is chosen for special effect, the horizontal measurement is still given first, as 12 x 9. The visual appeal of many formats is influenced by the selection of type face and size. Body copy and standard headlines should be set in the same type in every issue. Larger body type with some leading between the lines makes easier reading. A good, readable size is 9 point on the space of 10, or 10 on 12. Column width helps establish what size and leading look best.

Among the devices page designers can employ to package their content dramatically are rule boxes and Ben Day borders of from 4 to 12 points; Ben Day screens behind type to set it apart from other material; shifts in column width to emphasize a story; reverse type (white type reading out of a black background); large heading type, provocative wording and spacing, artistry in arrangement or design of letters to project a mood as well as communicate the word images; more white space around heads; larger, more dramatically cropped photos; outlined or specially screened photos; and drawings designed especially for the material and the space. All these are characteristic of magazine design.

Typography choices are determined largely by availability and by method of printing. Each printing house offers some variables as to face and size for body copy and headlines from which these basic decisions can be made. The staff has much more freedom with the other elements of design. Margins, column widths, folio design and placement, and heading style help establish the individuality of a publication. As much excitement in page design can be generated on newsprint as on the finest enamel stock.

Examples for study abound. The magazines displayed on newsstands offer suggestions for departmentalization and for page arrangement: news weeklies, special-interest monthlies, classic design quarterlies and annuals. The magazine supplements of the Sunday editions of metropolitan daily papers are worth examining. Private publications from organizations and major companies present some of the finest in magazine composition. College flyers, art-exhibit catalogues, annual reports, advertising brochures, and promotional pamphlets are often excellent pieces of graphic art. There is no reason a staff might not combine ideas gleaned through perusing several publications. Copying another printed piece in detail shows a lack of creativity, but adapting ideas of other publications to fit the limitations and possibilities of your own is a good beginning in developing creativity in graphics display. Through studying what professional page designers are doing, a student can become familiar with what makes good design. Those pages which fail to attract and hold attention should be studied for the reasons they are ineffective. Knowing what to avoid is equally as valuable as knowing what to emulate. Emulation, however, should be in the form of adaptation, not outright duplication. It is one thing to see an exciting design, change it here and there to better fit your use of it, and then execute a new version; it is quite another thing to trace something and tell yourself you are being creative. Cutting someone else's printed material and pasting it on your page "as is" surely is as much plagiarism as copying another's writing.

Creativity calls for individual expression. Creativity in communication means presenting understandable things in a different and striking way.

VARIATIONS OF FORMAT

Page sizes of magazines run from 5⅜ by 7½ in. (*Reader's Digest*) to 11½ by 17 (tabloid supplements of Sunday editions of metropolitan dailies). Paper stocks range from newsprint to 100-pound glossy enamel. By mid-1974 most national magazines had settled on an 8½ by 11-in. page as the most economical size. The small lithograph press currently prevalent in the printing industry makes an 8 x 10 page on a soft-finish white paper called offset vellum an economical choice for school publications. This format and the tabloid size on newsprint are equally popular in scholastic journalism. Another popular shape is the "short tab," 11 x 14½ in., which emulates the rotogravure magazines distributed with the Sunday papers. This 11-in. width can be structured with six 9½-pica columns, five 11-pica columns, four at 13 to 14½ picas, or three at 18 to 19½ picas. Many of the professional examples employ all these options at some time. Most publications specify a basic column structure for the bulk of the printed matter, and deviate from this measure for emphasis of special material. A page 66 picas wide can carry five columns at 11 picas, with 11 picas left to be distributed among the outside and inside margins and the white space between columns. National advertising for newspapers is often standardized on a 9½-pica column or 19-pica double column. Pages with advertising and copy can be laid out with one column measure for the ads and the balance of the space divided into another measure for the copy. On a 9 x 12 page, which normally has four 11-pica columns beside a 2-column ad running 19 picas, the remaining space is more attractively and economically utilized with two 13-pica columns of copy. Or the text may be set at 20 picas and indented at the left under 26-pica headings and subheads. It can make an attractive page to set copy at a measure different from the advertising next to it.

When the page size has been selected, column width can be determined by dividing the space that remains after the margins are set, or the margins may be set by subtracting from the total for columns and dividers. Dividing the page width into columns and margins may require some trial-and-error juggling to ascertain the best-looking and most workable arrangement. Once set, however, format specifications should call for absolute consistency in margins. Column widths are flexible; margins are not. There is no set rule for margin allotments, except that they are needed to frame the copy and give a unified effect to the full page. Artistically, pages seem to look better if the margins are not of equal width, and they seem more balanced if there is sufficient base to avoid a top-heavy feeling. The page size, column width, and typography have some influence on the most artistic spacing. Since the inside or "gutter" margin is doubled when two pages are viewed at once, this margin will probably be the narrower. In the old tradition, margins increased proportionately from the gutter around the top, outside, and to the largest measurement at the bottom. Dynamic graphics today often disregard this practice. Consider a 2-in. band of white at the top or a 1½-in. strip on the outside of the left-hand page. These generous margins can set off the page content dramatically. Placement of folio and departmental designations may be a factor in setting margin width.

Whatever decisions are made concerning margins, two rules hold: *(1)* better too much than too little (printed matter is better received and more easily read if generously framed in white space); and *(2)* never violate a margin with type (nothing should appear in the margin; illustrations either hold the marginal line or completely obliterate it by bleeding off the page edge. When the folio line is run "up the outside margin," in actuality the margin begins at the outside edge of that line of type and the balance of that line of type is kept "open" or unused. That is why a larger outside margin is needed when this folio placement is used.

The folio line includes the name of the publication, the date of issue, and the page number. These are usually found at the top of newspaper pages and at the bottom of newsmagazine pages. The complete information may appear together or may be divided in a variety of ways. Page numbers may appear at the top or bottom of a page and the other information in the opposite margin. For a double-page spread, the page numbers appear on each page, but the name of the publication and the date (including day, month, and year) could be split between the two pages. Department designations can appear as part of the folio or in a separate position. Folio lines need not be in especially large type, but they and the departmental identifiers should be consistent in appearance and placement, whether approached as design elements or utility components.

The cover of each issue need not be so similar as those of, say, *Time* or *U.S. News and World Report.* Such publications are vying with each other and dozens of other publications on crowded newsstands. Their constancy of appearance is their identifier. A school publication most often stands alone, and thus variety of cover design is of greater value than constancy. Consistency, however, is mandatory in the nameplate. The name of the publication should always look the same, though it may vary in size, placement, and even treatment. The nameplate must carry full information as to publication title; volume and issue number; day, date, and year; school; city, state, and zip code. True, national magazines do not carry "place of business" in their nameplates; they are national in scope, and no local tie-in is desired. School publications, by naming their institutions, have established a specific locale, and it needs further identification of city, state, and zip code. The United States is well populated with Thomas Jefferson high schools, Memorial high schools, and West high schools, and specification of the city and state completes the school identity. The volume and issue numbers on the cover and the folio information on inside pages are really more for the archivist than the reader. Those staffers charged with maintaining research files benefit from quick access to volume and issue notations on the cover. With widely spaced or sporadic publication schedules, the issue number on the front helps both reader and archivist know that they have the "next" issue and have not missed one. Such small details of format should be made to serve the publication and its immediate audience; that is their purpose. Those which have no function or make no contribution physically or aesthetically can be eliminated. Newsmagazines that limit themselves to a single large photograph on the cover of each issue are risking boredom in their audience. If, on the other hand, part of the contract with the printer is use of this standardization, then the staff must be alert for an exciting variety in photo techniques and content and must make an effort to include overprinted "teasers" announcing other content in the issue to help establish variety from issue to issue.

ESTIMATING THE COST

Setting the format is necessary before seeking bids from printers as to probable costs. This includes details of: page size, paper stock, basic column width, margins, sequence of content, style of folio placement, departmental designations, nameplate and a duplicate smaller version to appear in the masthead, the masthead itself, index or table of contents, headline styles, special treatments for editorials and standing columns, even minute decisions on style of cutlines and photo credits, by-lines, subheads, story breakers, and typographical endings.

The publication's budget and the availability of printer and paper are key factors in final selection of the basic format. Paper is turned out of the mills in standard sizes of sheets or rolls and in a number of grades of quality. Newsprint is among the lower-graded, less expensive papers milled in great quantity. Printing firms usually concentrate on a few grades and sizes of stock for the majority of their work, since each paper finish is matched with special-formula inks best suited to printing on it, and presses are designed to accommodate certain ranges of paper sizes. These equipment and inventory factors necessitate limitation in selection of quantity purchases by printers. Choosing special-order materials will make any job cost more than when the printer's standard materials are used.

Staffs contemplating a change should consult as many printers as possible, checking out all the possibilities of meeting the desired format. The quality of stock and the page size must be determined before a printer can estimate the cost of a job. Check as many printing possibilities as might be used for the magazine. If one printer does several publications in tabloid size on newsprint, there is a good probability of cashing in on a quantity-purchase discount. If offset vellum or glossy enamel stock in, say, 9 x 12 is preferred by the staff, then find a printer who has other clients using sizable quantities of that paper so that he will not have to buy small amounts of ink and paper just for one job. The staff that chooses an odd-size page or special paper must expect to pay special prices for a custom job and will probably waste a lot of paper in the trimmer.

The more detailed the format specifications of a proposed publication, the more accurate can be the printer's cost estimate. It is plausible to design or adjust a format within a particular shop's limitations. Most printers will gladly discuss the range of possibilities within their normal operations. Some may even be eager to contribute ideas in creative design. Most, however, prefer layouts and page structures that call for the least amount of makeready on their part. So it is up to the staff to establish a workable format with enough flexibility to permit creative and exciting display without undue stress on the shop's facilities. Letterpress printers offer the convenience of straight lines of type and neat pages because they work with strips or slugs of metal type and borders. The staff that uses letterpress does not have to furnish clean, camera-ready pages. Letterpress printing is less flexible, however; and because illustrations and trimmings must be cast in metal, cost and time are restraining factors on display effects. Offset printing is more widely used because of its greater availability and greater freedom in visual display; since entire pages are photographed and transferred to a single printing plate, variations in graphic design can be achieved with far less cost. The restrictions here rest with the staff's ability to cut and paste evenly and neatly. Crooked lines and slanting blocks of copy disturb the reader's eye and cause unfavorable reactions. When the printer does the paste-up and art pages, labor cost at the professional level is built into the charge. Offset estimates should clearly specify printing costs, with separate notations for camera-ready pages and for printer paste-up.

The budget should be established before a final decision is made to switch to newsmagazine format. The price of the product cannot exceed the ability to pay. In order to determine how much can be spent, a staff must assess its potential income. The first item to be entered would naturally be whatever subsidy is granted from the school board, activity fees, or other "outside" source. Adding to this a realistic appraisal of subscription or cash sales revenue establishes the basic amount available. When projected printing costs are determined, the balance of funds must come from advertising sales. If sale of advertising is not permitted, then costs must be held to the subsidy plus subscription. With no subsidy and/or no advertising, the cost must be held to whatever revenue can be expected. Planning to meet excess costs with bake sales or car washes is an unwise procedure, because the personnel of a publication's staff changes each year and interest in these extra activities should not form the criterion for journalistic participation.

When a feasible format has been selected and printers have submitted bids on cost per issue or per page, simple arithmetic will project the total annual cost. Equating this with the publication's expected annual income will quickly reveal whether a balanced budget can be achieved and how much money must be raised from advertising sales. Assuming that advertising is to be sold, the following formula is suggested for figuring a publication's budget:

Projected Annual Cost of Printing . . .	$AAAA.aa
Projected Annual Cost of Photography . .	BBB.bb
Other Expenses	CC.cc
Projected Total Annual Cost . . .	XXXX.xx
Subsidy (amount of gratis income) . . .	$ DDD.dd
Expectation from Sales (realistic) . . .	EEEE.ee
Projected Total Income	$YYYY.yy

Total annual cost (X) minus total income (Y) equals annual deficit (Z)—the amount needed to be raised by sale of advertising.

Meeting the Budget

To determine whether the required revenue from sales of advertising can be obtained, the staff must appraise the availability of space to sell, the merchants who will buy, and the price the market will bear for each inch or block of advertising space. The amount of space a publication has for sale and the amount of monetary return that can be expected are interdependent; the less space open for ads, the higher the cost of that space must be. A workable rule of thumb for figuring the amount of space available for advertising is to divide the total number of pages in an issue by ⅓ or ¼, since this is the usual percentage of ad space carried in a school publication. To be sure you have ¼ to ⅓ of the space available for sale, block out the number of pages that definitely will not carry ads, the cover, editorial-viewpoint page(s), and whatever special-feature or news pages the staff designates (often the center spread and the back cover.) One half of the remaining space should correspond to near ⅓ of the total, because, except for single large ads, advertising space should not exceed half of each page on which advertising appears. The editorial staff should not block out for non-ad pages space that is needed to meet the budget.

Ads can be sold by the portion of a page, as for most school yearbooks, or by the column inch, as for most newspapers. If portions of a page are used, they should be converted into column inches for comparative pricing, an important factor in setting rates. Consider the price the competition is receiving for advertising space. Commercial publications have printed rate cards available on request. Then evaluate the return an advertiser can expect from placement in each publication. The staff should conduct a survey each year or so to determine the spending habits and the volume of the school market. With statistics on how much money students spend or influence the spending of and where that money goes, the staff can substantiate claims of potential return for advertising dollars spent and probably can command prices for its space equal to or higher than that of the competition.

To convert the ¼ or ⅓ total space for advertising into column inches, measure the number of column inches on a single page and

Visual Impact 41

multiply by half the number of pages that will carry advertising. Again, the total number of column inches for advertising should be no more than half of each page designated as an ad page. The larger the number of pages in an issue, the more pages can be reserved as non-ad.

Example: a 16-page, 8 x 10 newsmagazine with three 9-in. columns per page will carry 27 column in. per page for a total of 432 in. Block out the cover, pages 2 and 3, 8 and 9, and 16; this leaves 10 ad pages. At ½ each, the yield for ads is a total of (27 × 10 ÷ 2 =) 135 column in. Dividing the total of 432 column in. by 3 gives 144 in. as the suggested amount of space for advertising; dividing by 4 sets 108 in. as the "minimum." The 135 in. projected above falls comfortably within this range. For a 12-page issue, the total inches come to 324. Eight pages will probably be needed to carry the ads. Blocking out 4 pages, then, leaves 8 half-pages for ads, or 108 in., which is ⅓ of the total space. In a paper this size, ¼ would probably be too small a percentage to pay out. And when advertising will not bring sufficient return per inch to pay out, the percentage of space devoted to ads may have to be increased to half or more.

When the total projected income (Y) is subtracted from the total projected cost (X) and the amount to be raised from advertising (Z) is determined, then the cost per inch can be figured. In the example above, the total annual inches available would be 135 multiplied by the number of issues used in projecting the annual cost (X). This sum divided into the annual deficit (Z) will give a reasonable figure for pricing column inches of advertising. Assuming that (A), total cost of printing, was projected at $500 per issue for 12 issues (every three weeks), the total printing cost would be $6,000. If photography and miscellaneous expenses combined added up to another $600, and if "gratis" income is, say, $500, with projected subscription sales at 1,200 ($2.50 each) netting $3,500 income, the problem would read:

$$\begin{array}{r} X\ (\$6{,}600\text{—total cost}) \\ -Y\ (\ 3{,}500\text{—total income without ads}) \\ \hline Z\ (\$3{,}100\text{—deficit: ad budget} \end{array}$$

Ad inches per issue (135) times the number of issues (12) yields 1,620 in. for sale annually in this problem. With $3,100 ÷ 1,620, the price is $1.91 per in. Ads for this budget should not be sold for less than $2.50 per column inch, because the total ad space is not likely to be sold for every issue. If 135 in. cannot be sold for each issue, the realistic figure should be multiplied by the number of issues, that figure divided into the deficit (Z), and the resulting higher price should be asked. If subscriptions will not bring $2.50 or 1,200 cannot be sold, those figures must be adjusted to fit the actual situation.

The formula: Total cost minus income without ads equals deficit: ad budget. This deficit: ad budget divided by total inches available for sale equals lowest price per inch at which ads can be sold. When a workable budget has been figured, the staff should enter into a written contractual agreement with the printer. This contract should stipulate not only the costs of printing, but time factors, quality of work expected of both parties, and other considerations that might hinder the effectiveness on either side.

Once the staff has a format and a printer who can execute it at a price that can be met, the creative side of journalism can proceed.

There should always be understanding and clear communication between the business staff and the editorial staff. Each must respect the other's role in the production of the publication. Each must meet its own responsibilities. Ad space is sacred and not to be violated for editorial use. Yet ad space must be sold, and it is the responsibility of the business staff to fill its quota. The editorial staff justifiably resents having to bump good stories to accommodate late-arriving ads. By the same token, they have every right to resent having to fill ad holes when the business staff falls down. Cooperation, adjustability, and a supply of good copy on hold serve well in such emergency situations. When business and editorial staffs work together, communicating regularly and realizing the other's needs, a good business experience can be realized.

The publication staff that can operate independently of administrative subsidy enjoys the satisfactions of self-support and can take extra pride in their accomplishments while acquiring additional skills and professional experience.

Visual Impact

To summarize, the staff enjoying the benefits of publishing a newsmagazine will need:

1. A fully detailed format with rigid rules for basic structure, but with flexibility to allow considerable variety in page design.
2. A complete range of heading type to offer sufficient variety within the standard schedule plus additional display-type selections for special designs.
3. A good understanding of the format possibilities and an agility with creative design.
4. A solid understanding of costs and obligations and how to meet them.
5. An efficient and energetic business staff as well as a dedicated and creative editorial staff, both with the ability to work together with mutual respect and a common goal.

Chapter III

GRAPHICS DESIGN

Some of the examples exhibited in this chapter are included for special techniques or devices employed, others were selected for heading style or typography, still others for the use of more than one element. Their variety attests to the diversity of good format and page design open to the school publication.

    Designing pages is, for some, one of the most exciting activities in working on student publications. Newsmagazine format offers greater freedom in the presentation of information, and that freedom usually returns a greater interest in the subject matter from the readers. Since pages are smaller, often a whole page can be devoted to a single story of major importance so that the informative copy, the attention-getting type, and the bold illustrations can be arranged on the white space to give that extra dimension: visual impact.
    Once the complete format has been settled upon, the creative aspects of designing within that format can begin. The ability to visualize finished pages of type, illustrations, and white space can be acquired through practice. It involves creating an attractive and functional composition when arranging on the white space the blocks of body type, illustrations, larger heading type, and smaller fragments of type such as subheads, story breakers, and cutlines.

ELEMENTS OF DESIGN

    A formula for achieving impact in a layout begins with asymmetrical balance from a minimum of visual units arranged into some continuous form, anchored with a dynamic focal point, and spiced with sufficient contrasts to achieve interest. An uncluttered, free-flowing design can be achieved by grouping various elements within the given area in such a way that organization results. Elements are in some way merged with other(s), and the total number of elements becomes fewer while these collective groups emerge as larger elements. The placing of a screened background behind a story and its headline reduces the number of elements on that page by making all parts of the head and the story into one element. Boxing a story, head, and illustration reduces all of these to one element. Not all elements in a design will necessarily blend with their neighbors. Some will forcefully stand apart in contrast. Those which are similar enough to merge should pose, as a group, strong contrast with other material. Good design is built on achieving balance through the principles of conformity and contrast anchored with concentration on one major focal point. Columns of body type are individual lines of identical small type grouped into one visual element. When aligned top or bottom with other columns, they form yet another "group" and create a vertical pattern. Contrasting rows of body type with bold horizontal headlines spread wide across the page is characteristic of newsmagazine page design. The impact of clashing directions attracts the reader's eye.

In *Design with Type,* Carl Dair lists seven dimensions of concord and contrast that can be employed to create effective typographical design: size, weight, structure, form, texture, direction, and color. Structure can be interpreted as the organizational pattern or design of an element, form as the shapes of separate elements, and texture as a pattern created by groupings or inherent in some element. Of these principles, Dair says, size is the primary performer. The grouping of small elements to form larger shapes exemplifies this. Adding other elements of contrast and holding the design together with points of harmony make for good page composition. Typeface structures and forms, sizes and weights offer opportunities for injecting contrast and accord. They may serve either purpose, but should not be paired when they create conflict. Contrast must be sharp. If contrast is too subtle, conflict will result. When two pictures are close together in a layout and one is lower than the other by the space of only a line or two of type, there is discord. A near-miss results in disharmony. Placing the two photos on the same horizontal plane will restore harmony. Increasing the space by which they do not align will offer contrast. Size and weight of elements in a design call for the same consideration. Neither a single element nor the sum of the parts should overbalance the space allowed.

What happens to the white space is as important to a design as is the arrangement of the other elements. Characteristic of magazine pages is a greater use of white space. There is not the demand to fill every corner and all the space between. More "air" is injected around the elements and between the lines. These more open pages promote both reader interest and reader convenience. Often the white space is used, free-form, as part of the design, flowing on the page, directing the eye from one element to the next, and coercing the reader to consume the entire layout. At other times, the white area is spaced or margined in even strips to frame the head and body type and set one story apart from another. Old-style newspaper printers would air out text that did not fill the column by adding space between the lines of the last few paragraphs, making this material appear different from the preceding paragraphs and making it more difficult to read. Good magazine design calls for keeping the text in blocks and grouping the white space around the headline and/or other display type. As a general rule, extra space is more effective at the top of the page than at the bottom. White space at the bottom appears to be a mistake on someone's part—a lack of planning. With real planning and a knowledge of counting copy before it is set in type, there should be little problem with leftover white space. It is a good practice to begin making up a page at the bottom.

Alignment of like elements, whether in close proximity or not, is one principle of unity that lends much to organization of a design. Just as lines of type in a column are aligned (set flush) to form an illusionary rectangle, the same effect of neatness can be achieved by lining up other elements to create balance. Eye travel has been touted by psychologists as the essential consideration for persons attempting to communicate through print. The designer can compel the eye to follow an imaginary line by injecting reinforcers to continue the form. The imaginary contour should never carry the eye out of the space, but keep directing it within the design. In aligning elements to create continuous form, three strong points should never appear in a straight line that might send the attention out of the design unless a forceful stopper is injected to redirect attention within the layout. The "magic" effect of closure can be achieved in a graphics design by placing the three points in a triangle with no side parallel to the rectangular lines of the layout or page. Another area of conformity is rhythm. Repeating elements can establish a rhythm and weave a background pattern that adds dimension to the accents. The rhythm created by repeating a striking folio or departmental designators performs as a subtle bass clef for the dramatic melody in special layout pages. Consistency in small details, organized contrasts of significant elements, and planned visual surprises of unusual treatment collaborate to effect good rhythm in a design.

It is these principles of contrast and conformity, playing against each other to attract attention, direct the eye, and maintain interest, which serve as props for typographical designers. With practice, makeup artists learn to manipulate their puzzle pieces to achieve a balance of contrast and conformity to construct finished pages that establish the mood or tone of the printed material, pages that could project these characteristics of emotion even if the language were foreign.

Designing Pages

In planning any layout, the first consideration should be the nature of the material and the audience—the purpose to be accomplished. Straight news calls for an honest, no-nonsense presentation; editorial material demands dignity coupled with appeal and credibility; sports pages certainly should convey action; and so it goes. Student page designers have their greatest freedom to experiment with feature, humor, and literary pages. Here again, all pages including covers should be designed to reflect the overall tone or philosophy of the publication. With "far out" graphics, readers expect contemporary thought and attitudes.

In selecting a design for a story, its location and relationship to other elements in the publication will set the general tone. Beyond considerations of the departmental influence, other elements on the page that will be competing for attention must be considered. With large, forceful advertising alongside, story matter will gain attention by contrast if sedately displayed with simple heading and text arrangement, no fancy boxes, a minimum of subheading, and yet with sufficient white space to avoid density or a heavy appearance. On the other hand, alongside a grouping of small ads, a single large, forceful arrangement with screened background, partial or rounded box, or exaggerated indentation of body type coupled with some strong and striking heading type will unify the whole page and save it from cluttered anonymity.

When two or more stories are to occupy a single page, and especially when two such pages face each other as a spread, it is imperative to formulate cluster patterns that will appear unified yet give each separate portion its due emphasis. Here screens, borders, various headline forms, and blank space can serve to separate, while the principles of alignment, repetition, continuation of form, and grouping of similar units help unify and provide organization. A collection of news briefs is a case in point. Small stories with individualized headlines scattered about a page produce clutter. The same stories set in equal measure, headlined with the same type, and arranged in a repeat pattern will project a unified appearance. Boxed or screened, the collection will become an attractive whole representing a single design element.

Pages to be designed fall into several categories: covers, special-story pages, editorial and comment pages, standing departmental pages, and pages with advertising. In some formats sports pages command special attention, and so does the back cover at times. The sequence usually remains the same from issue to issue, and departmental features with and without advertising may take on some similarity if layout variances are fairly well restricted by advertising placement and/or standing column headings. This should not be an area of concern, because there is plenty of room for creativity in other areas, and some semblance of repetition in minor areas keeps the readers familiar with their favorite sections of the publication, assuming, of course, that what is repeated is good design in the first place.

COVERS

Cover designs demand careful attention to detail and all the flair you can muster. Covers should always relate to inside content in some way. One of the more popular practices is to focus on the lead story with a single photo or a layout or drawing that illustrates the story or sets its mood. Sometimes a larger or smaller version of the art on the inside page is reproduced on the cover. If the issue has a thematic approach with several stories pertaining to one general subject area, then this theme should be established on the cover. If the issue has, on the other hand, several "big guns" and a composite layout is not feasible, then the most dramatic one might be depicted on the cover and "teasers" (lines of type calling attention to other stories) incorporated into the cover design. Bold, simplified designs in the poster technique are very popular choices. Publications of 16 or more pages usually have an index or table of contents. Sometimes the cover announcement of important content can be made through placement of the index on the cover.

It is a good idea to study an entire magazine display on the newsstands and decide what basic style of cover design best suits the tone and philosophy of your publication. Some will appear too busy, others too plain. It is your readers' right to expect some continuity as well as a generous measure of variety in your cover designs. The nameplate should always look the same, a clear reproduction of the *original* art. The size and placement may well vary from one issue to the next, but the design should not change. This design should be an impact item in itself. It should be distinctive and unusual enough for the reader to remember it, but it should not be so ornate or cluttered as to make reading it difficult, nor so large as to overpower the content. Hand-drawn nameplates generally lack the class required. Hand-set press-on type can produce a much neater design unless a professional artist is available.

Whatever the design of the cover, framing deserves careful attention. Bleed photographs with type overburned or reversed into the "dead" areas are very popular. Dead areas of photos are those portions with no significant features—dispensable spots that can be covered over without detracting from the message of the picture. When used to carry type, dead areas should be fairly even in tone; type is difficult to read when surprinted or reversed over much tonal gradation. When the illustration does not bleed, it will be more effective if bordered in some way. Plenty of line borders are available to frame pictures or layouts. The plain black line is probably the most effective. Bleed borders of black or shaded gray make good frames. Fancy hand-drawn borders usually look less polished and are a weak choice. The cover design, like the nameplate, should be as crisp and free of unnecessary marks as possible.

Framing enhances the crispness through definition of the area. White space aids readability, adds class, and should control the reader's eye pattern. Yet both are secondary in page design. The reader should be unaware of them, because they serve to direct attention to the reading matter and illustrations. For this reason, borders should not overpower the material contained inside, and there should be not so much white space on a page that the reader suspects the staff failed to plan ahead or the writers failed to complete the story.

The back cover should be designed with special care, because, as often as not, the publication will be placed face down. If this space is sold for advertising, it should command a much higher price than the same amount of space inside. Often the back cover is devoted to sports and given bold, dramatic design. Other schools find this the ideal spot for special in-depth reports or interpretive articles. The dictates of your format will influence the display style of the back cover.

Inside Pages

There is no set formula for designing pages without advertising save the observing of margins. Standard column width can be discarded in favor of other measures suited to the material; type may even be set in unusual shapes or a different size. When more than one story is to occupy a page, or when it is desirable to distinguish between stories on facing pages, one article may be boxed or surprinted over a screened background. An aid in distinguishing one from another is a shift in measure or placement, such as using three columns in the space of four, or four on five. Varying heading arrangement also serves to separate type blocks. When sideheads are used, especially in the middle of the page, it is important to box them, either all the way around, or just at top and bottom in what is called a sideless box. Sideless boxes are more frequently used with Ben Day or shaded borders in at least 4 points and often up to 12 points in thickness. Background screens are like solid boxes and do not need additional borders to set them off from the rest of the page. Type will look better if indented on each side when surprinted on a screen, allowing a pica of screen framing all around, including above the head and at the bottom.

Center Spread

When working with the center spread, ignore what would be the gutter margins and consider the entire space as one page, which it actually is—one single sheet of paper, horizontal in shape. If a division is desired, such as setting the editorials apart from some other feature(s), the center margin or a portion of the white divider can be moved to any spot desired. Suppose a publication is 9 x 12, making the center spread 18 x 12; if only 20 picas at the far left is dedicated to editorial material, and the rest is to contain a feature story that the staff does not want confused with the sanction or policy of the magazine, a wide white area of 3 to 5 picas can be placed between the editorials and the feature story. The separation will be quite plain, and the longer story can be laid out in the remaining 75 or so picas with maximum effectiveness.

The few inside pages that do not carry advertising will be open for creative display. It is hoped that most will be devoted to a single story and given as much photographic assistance as possible. People like pictures, the larger the better. Professor Edmund C. Arnold of Syracuse University, a prominent typographical expert, admonishes students to make photos a column wider than originally intended, to crop ruthlessly and dramatically. When a choice must be made between more or larger pictures, opt for larger. One good photo for a story is better than several smaller ones, as a general rule. It takes courage and conviction to amputate a person's ears in bringing the photo up larger while holding the space to the width allotted, but facial features thus enlarged have more dramatic impact than a smaller version of the entire head.

Advertising

For all pages that are to carry advertising, the first consideration is to dummy in the ads. In professional publications the ad dummy is prepared first and sent to the editorial department. The space not occupied by paid advertisements is termed the "news hole." The "editorial department" refers to the editor and staff who deal with all material in the publication not paid for by advertisers. This includes news, features, columns, and pictorial matter in addition to viewpoint material. Once the ads are dummied in, page designers can set about placing the other content.

In arranging the advertisements on the pages for magazine layout, the ads are grouped by like sizes and kept to the bottom or outside columns of the pages. Do not pyramid ads on small pages; it creates a newspaper appearance that is out of character. The ideal situation is for all advertisements to be placed adjacent to reading matter, avoiding "bumping" illustrations or boxes, although sometimes it can't be done. Ads should be boxed and set in different type faces from text matter and headlines that will appear nearby. Borders should be designed with restraint and not too much variety. It is distracting when several ads with wild borders are grouped together and appear to be fighting for the reader's attention. One solution to this problem, which has been popular with a number of school publications recently, is the use of a single borderline to separate ads, rather than boxing each ad separately and thereby having double borders when two ads meet. Use of the single line also ensures that all ads are boxed uniformly, and a tone of dignity is added with the additional air. When the preferred situation applies, where one single large ad occupies part of a page, makeup artists should remember that ads should complement the pages. Combine loud ads with quiet text and vice versa. Just as ads should not bump other attention-getting material such as boxes and cuts, so they should not fight with heavily displayed stories. If there is illustrative matter with a story on a page where ads will run, then nonpictorial ads are the wiser choice. By the same token, pictorial ads can brighten a page where the reading matter is rather plain. Dignity and readability should be the goals for makeup personnel.

Learning to make up a page not only involves knowing the rudiments of page layout and acquiring a repertoire of skills in manipulating the components to achieve the most effective design. It also requires a working knowledge of typography and picture proportioning (see Chapter IV) and a concept of spacing. This means that page designers can figure how to fit copy—to make an accurate appraisal of the number of lines of type a piece of copy will require when set in a given size and face at a specific line length. It means that persons involved with writing headlines and making up pages must know the exact count for each unit of a headline and the amount of space that should be allowed for same. It means knowing how to find the usable picture in a photographic print and eliminate extraneous portions, then to figure the space that picture will occupy when reduced or enlarged in reproduction.

FORMAT TYPOGRAPHY

Since the page designer must have a thorough knowledge of the possibilities and restrictions of all the type included in the publication's format, every publication must have a complete typographical schedule. This includes elements of the basic format such as standardization on one size and face for body copy, consistent spacing between the lines of body text, a regular column width for the bulk of the material, and selection of standard type for the headlines, for cutlines, and for other special lines of type such as subheads, story breakers, standing column heads, folio lines, departmental identifiers, even by-lines and photo credits. Consistency in typography for these recurring fragments of type is an element of reinforcement that keeps the reader aware of the individuality of a publication. It establishes a familiarity that breeds acceptance.

A large poster should be displayed on the wall of the lab area showing the sizes of types to be used and the unit count per pica or per column for each sample. Whether the headlines are numbered, as is done for newspaper design, or keyed in some other fashion such as specifying use—news, features, sports, editorials, and the like— is incidental. It is important that all persons who assign or write heads be familiar with character counting and the amount of space a headline will consume, and with the specific symbols and notations their printer prefers for marking instructions.

There is a set of "universal" copy- and proofreading marks that most printers understand. Yet there are variations used by some printing houses, and it is always a good idea to have a thorough understanding of the printer's preferences. Instructions for typesetting and placement and special treatments must be fully understood. Make sure your printer will interpret your instructions the way you think you wrote them.

Each staff member who is involved in marking instructions for the typesetter, in writing headlines, and in designing or pasting up pages should have a copy of the complete typographical schedule for the publication. Once the format is set for standard usages in body text, column width, spacings, margins, and typographical devices, then the creative designers can vary from the norm for special effect, calling sometimes for wider columns, larger type sizes, or special shapes for particular pieces of copy. The complete schedule should include the most commonly used variations from the standard. If a publication is on a 3-column format, for instance, the chart will certainly show the type size and number of characters per line for this spacing, but should also include character count for use of two columns and other variations that might be used recurringly. *Note:* This involves redistributing the space *within* the margins. Margin areas do not change; they are always the same on every page.

For example, if the print area (space inside margins) across a page totals 39 picas, which are usually divided into three 12-pica columns with 1½-pica spacing between, and the layout calls for two columns, then the 39 picas can be divided into two 18½-pica columns with 2 picas between. Another apportionment of the space might be to use a box or a screened background for two 18-pica columns separated by a single pica. The two remaining picas will be needed outside each column for the box rule or the frame of background screen.

Counting Copy

All copy should be counted as to the number of lines it will occupy in a specific type size at a given measure (column width). The printer needs to know the exact type and size and line length before he can set the material. Specify the full name of the typeface, the point size, the slug size (the amount of leading,) and the line length in picas—as 10/12 Century Bold x 18. Or write across the top of the first page: Set at 18 picas Century Bold 10/12. The staff should record the measure and length of each piece of copy on a "slug sheet," once the copy is readied for the typesetter. This record, along with notations of finished size for each illustration, is used for writing headlines and drawing preliminary page layouts while the copy is at the shop. Most professional publications plan their display before sending any copy to a typesetter. The editors know exactly how many inches or lines are best for a design, and type specifications insure that the copy will fit the layout and spacing planned. If a story is to occupy a single page, the pros will not send much more copy for that story than a page can hold, including heads and illustrations. In any case, it should not be a hit-or-miss situation of hoping the typeset material will fit or fill after it comes from the print shop. Careful counting beforehand can facilitate making up pages and also avoid wasting money on unused type. Killed copy costs, too.

Counting copy can be simplified for the staff if the reporters use standard pica or elite typewriters. Some of the newer, more sophisticated electronic machines produce printed material that is inconsistent in character spacing. Such machines are fine for other uses, but they complicate character counting for estimating the length of typeset matter. To determine the number of lines a piece of copy will require when set in a given size at specified measure, the person counting must first know the usual number of characters that type size (and face) takes for the specified line length. The process can be simplified if the print shop provides a table of character count per pica for each face and size. If not, some staffer who is comfortable with mathematics can draw up a chart by the following method for body type:

Take a known sample of the type in correct size and spacing between words and with the desired amount of leading between lines. Count at least a dozen full lines (lines that appear to have as many characters as the line will hold, as opposed to lines where the machine has added space between words or characters to achieve a line flush with all others in that block). Give each character and

Graphics Design

space one count. With a dozen samples of full lines counted, add them and divide by 12 to determine the average line count. Round out to the nearest whole number, and call that the number of characters per line at that measure. Then lay a ruler vertically on the type sample block and count the number of lines per inch or whatever measurement you will be using in your publication.

With the character count per line and the number of lines per inch determined, take a piece of copy that is ready for the typesetter and measure across the page to the number of characters in a full line of set type. Pica typewriters print 10 characters to the inch, and elite typewriters print 12. A 6-inch line, then, in pica type will contain 60 characters. If a single line of typed copy holds two lines of typeset matter (in this example a "set" line would hold 30 characters and a typewriter line, 60), then the number of lines can be determined by doubling the count on the number of lines in the typewriter copy. When copy has been typed in such a way that one line of copy will make one and a fraction lines of set text, draw a pencil line lightly down the page at the point where the character count equals that of a set line. Sum up the leftover line fragments, allowing for spaces between words, one line at a time to equal the character count of a set line; then total the sum of the full fragment lines and the sum of the whole lines. (Partial lines at the end of paragraphs must be counted as full lines because they occupy the depth of a whole line.) Adding up the parts to equal a full-line count may be easier if scored one paragraph at a time. Now, divide the total line count for the entire piece of copy by the number of lines of set type per inch to obtain the number of inches the copy will require in its finished state.

Copy may also be estimated by character total for standard and variable-space typewriters. If it is not possible to determine the character count of a line by using a ruler, then count the first few lines, allowing one count for every character and space. Gauge the average line count for the typed copy, and consider this average as the count for each line, including the fragmentary lines ending paragraphs. Count these fragments as whole lines, because set type will also have paragraph end fragments. Multiply the number of lines in the copy by the number of characters in the average line; this will give the total characters for the entire piece. Then divide the total character count by the number of characters per line in the type size and measure to be used. This will reveal the number of lines of type for the copy. Divide this line total by the number of lines per inch, and you have the space required to print that copy.

Example: Average line count in typewriter copy—63
Average line count in set text type—38
Number of lines of typewriter copy—115
Number of lines per inch in set type—7

63 x 115 = 7,245 characters in copy
7,245 ÷ 38 = 190.7 (or 191) lines of type
191 ÷ 7 = 27 inches plus three lines (27½ inches) total space.

It should not take much pencil pushing to convince student editors that all copy should come to the desk typed at a specific, easy-to-figure measure. The easiest to use, for both copy counters and copywriters, is material typed at the same or double the measure for a line of set type. If the character count for the average line of set body text at the standard column width is 35, then typed copy should be prepared at a 70-character line. Then copy counters can assess quickly the number of lines and determine the amount of space required for that piece on the finished page. When type is to be set at an unusual measure, if the writer knows ahead of time and can type the copy at that measure (or double it if lines are too short for ease of typing), much time can be saved in the copy-fitting process. One more reason why professionals preplan in minute detail; it not only saves time, but also gives a much more polished look to the finished product.

Copy comes back from the typesetter in solid blocks unless preplanning has dictated a special shape or contour for it. To have type "wrap" an illustration—follow the outline of the drawing or design—careful counting and marking instructions for the printer must precede sending the copy to the shop. If copy is to be reversed—printed white on a dark background—the type size should be larger than for regular body copy or set in boldface. The greater the amount of reverse copy, the larger the type size need be. The human eye is trained to read black on white. Too much reverse type proves to be a burden that the eye will often reject. Also, if the typeface has very thin lines, the camera may lose these in processing. The eye may also reject surprinted type—black type printed over a photo or drawing. There is no problem with a plain gray screen, but the reader may rebel at trying to decipher type over an irregular pattern if there is much to read. It is preferable to surprint or overprint the type in a fairly constant portion or dead area of the picture such as the sky, the street, or the side of a building rather than over trees or grass or other areas where dark and light appear in busy little patches.

HEADLINES

Headlines or titles must fit in two ways; of course, the space must accommodate them physically, but they also should be appropriate to the content and mood of the copy in words and appearance. In magazine format, headings need not always be in newspaper style. They can be titles or questions or whatever best piques the reader's attention and interest. Headings are a part of the whole presentation and not necessarily a summary of the content. Quite often the physical appearance of a headline is an integral part of the design and conveys the message visually as well as verbally. Special typefaces or special treatment of regular faces can contribute. On Valentine's Day, the Houston *Post* used its standard front-page nameplate inserting small solid hearts for the three o's in the name. No further message was needed; no explanation was required.

Styles of headlines for use in newsmagazines are limited only by the publication's print shop or the staff's creative ability. Such standard practices as using kickers (overlines of smaller type that help to clarify the headline) or hammers (side or overlines of larger type that lead into or establish the basic thought of the headline per se), and breaking boxes with headlines offer visual relief from straight news-type headlines. Creative typography can produce headlines that enhance communication either through the arrangement of the type or the appropriateness of its special design to the mood of the story. Some interesting ways to arrange type involve: (1) placing multiline heads to the side of the story, flush left or flush right, or all lines centered, (2) floating lines of varying length artistically in the space allowed, dividing into lines that sound right rather than come out to special measure, (3) using more than one size of type in longer heads, emphasizing important words, (4) arranging lines to follow the contour of the text or illustration at either side, or (5) dropping the head into a well framed by body text. Some single line heads read into, read out of, or run through the text; some stand on end or run up the side and across the top of the type block. Sometimes heads are carved out of one edge of the photograph, or are incorporated into the illustration. Some run at the bottom of the page. Placement of heads other than over the story should be reserved for occasions when the composition is so well set off from other material that the reader has no difficulty connecting headline and story. Whenever the headline does not precede the text, some piece of display—a subhead, the by-line, or a large initial letter—should be used at the top of the first paragraph to establish the opening.

Headline type can be reversed, overburned on a dead area of the illustration, boxed, or screened. Letters can be arranged to touch or overlap one another to form a design, to reflect themselves in reverse, in words that repeat in a rhythmic pattern or words that convey moods either by their arrangement or typographical design. Letters simulating stars-and-stripes bunting tend to signify "government," "Uncle Sam," "federal," and "patriotic" tones or subject matter. Such type would hardly be appropriate for antiestablishment material unless readers would grasp the satire. Type arranged to bunch up at the end of the line, especially if the wording suggests impact, can convey contact and add to the forcefulness of a football story.

Deviations from the printer's standard type offerings are limited to the outside availability of transfer type and the staff's ability to purchase and use same. Letterpress publications are restricted by the rigidity of metal type and its bases and by the necessity of having engravings made for artistic designs. Offset printing permits more flexibility within its cost. A number of companies produce letters on acetate that can be transferred to paper by rubbing one letter at a time. Sheets of this so-called cold type cost from $2 to $5. The letters come in a wide range of faces and sizes and are available in larger communities at commercial art-supply houses. Many college and university bookstores carry some selection of transfer type. Catalogues with samples of the varieties designed by each firm are usually distributed free by dealers who carry the line. Manufacturers will advise school publication staffs where their products can be purchased and will provide catalogues. When acetate or rub-on type is used, designs can be created with the letters, or typefaces can be employed that contribute to the mood of the headline and reflect the thrust of the story. Mood type such as letters with frost or snow on top to introduce something cool has long been used in advertising, and such designs are now popular among magazine page designers. These art-type selections, while they do add much interest and excitement to the pages, are somewhat expensive and their effectiveness needs to be judged in this light. If too much variance is used in heading type through a publication, some of the stability of consistency will be sacrificed. Special-effect types will have more impact if saved for those times when their use is warranted by the importance of the content with which they are applied. Appropriateness of design to the use is a necessary factor in effectiveness. Script or Old English letters add no excitement to sports pages. A strong, bold standard type better carries sports stories.

Counting headlines, since the type is larger, requires more precision. Although newsmagazine heads are not required to fill a specific width, nor to contain two lines of near equal length, persons involved with writing heads must know the limitations. Counting characters is still necessary to assure fitting all that needs to be said into the space allowed. The standard unit allotment is one count for all characters and spaces except that M and W count 2; all other caps count 1½; and i and 1 count ½. Using this standard, count a known sample of a given typeface and size to set the maximum count for each column width in a publication. If the print shop offers a characters-per-pica chart, much time can be saved; if not, once figured, the headline schedule can be posted for all to use. This system works for most art typefaces, but some, with unusual spacings, need to be measured for the specific combination of words to be used in the space. Special-design heads may be written first for greatest effect with words, then fitted to the space through type selection. The freedom in magazine head writing is that the wording is more important than the line spacing. With more room allotted and no requirement to fill a specific column measure, the type can be made to serve the message rather than the reverse.

PREPLANNING

The publications that are most successful at achieving top-quality design consistently are those that are preplanned, those for which the editors have a special layout in mind at the time story and photo assignments are made. These publications work with a futures book, in which story ideas are set up months ahead; they have the extra touch of editorial board planning in detail beforehand. The staff members maintain a backlog of good copy, ready or working, and have specific ideas for layouts on such copy before time for typesetting. When the photographer is aware of the spacing and use planned for pictures on an assignment, the results are more likely to fulfill the editor's expectations. That does not mean that all photographic coverage should be shot to fit a preconceived layout. When this does work out, fine. But when circumstances on a shooting assignment do not turn out as anticipated, whether for the better or the worse, the makeup staff should have the ability to capitalize on the best aspects of the pictures that materialize. Sometimes adjustments to availability prove to be more interesting than the original plan. It is that in preplanning the page designer has become familiar with the elements to be placed and can manage adjustments with dexterity. Constant practice at designing pages will reinforce this ability with a multiplicity of variables to draw upon.

One of the first steps in page designing is to memorize the space measurements involved: full-page dimensions, margins, column widths and spacings, and typographical variables. Coupled with the ability to manipulate illustrative material through cropping, reducing, and enlarging, these skills serve as tools for precision. The flair for dramatic design must be developed and is needed for adding excitement to special pages and covers. Not all persons on a staff will attain this special knack, but most can master the techniques of laying out the general formula pages for most publications. Since many pages probably contain advertising and/or standing columns, it is a matter

Graphics Design 63

of familiarity with the standard space dimensions and the publication's basic format for the bulk of the page makeup.

The Sketch Dummy

The sketch dummy comes in two forms, the thumbnail sketch and the actual-size preliminary draft. In either case, a series of symbols is employed to indicate large type, body text, art ("cuts"), and typographical specifications ("type specs"). Wavy lines are used to indicate headlines and run horizontally across the entire space reserved for each head. Body text is indicated by vertical lines which often wave, but more gently than those indicating headlines. These vertical lines begin where the text is to begin and run down that column to the point where the story either ends or continues to the adjacent column. If continuing, the line curves up to the next column and continues to go down and back up until all columns to be occupied by that copy block are scored vertically. When the terminal point is reached for that piece of reading matter, an arrow point is made at the end of the line. This means the copy follows the line all the way to "here." Pictures, cartoons, drawings, and combinations of these are indicated by rectangles boxing the space to be occupied. Most sketch artists place an X in these rectangles, although some consider a single diagonal line sufficient. Advertisements are shown by rectangles of appropriate size, with "ad" written in the space and, preferably, the name of the advertiser (Consumer Prod. Ad or JACKS Ad, etc.). In full-scale sketch dummies, the headlines are often written in or key words are used to identify the story. Headline type size and face are indicated either by numbered key from the head schedule or by actual name such as Futura Bold 36 (pt.) or Tempo Ital. 24 (pt.) followed by the slug line or topic of the story. Cutlines are indicated by straight horizontal lines in the space the cutline will occupy, not necessarily the number of lines that will occupy the space, but, as nearly as possible, the same width.

Using the thumbnail sketch, proportioned to the page (or spread) dimensions, page designers can experiment with arrangements of the various elements to find the most effective pattern. After all the "rules" have been observed, it is still "what looks best" with the specific material that influences the final decisions. Working within the miniature space helps to simplify the design. It forces grouping of elements, visualizing the structural form, and defining the center of gravity or dominant element.

Grouping of elements into single visual units helps avoid clutter. It establishes order. To add interest it is necessary to employ contrast, so groupings must contrast with other groupings or single elements, especially in relationship to size, weight, and/or direction. White spaces, likewise, must break monotony with inequality. Balance cannot be achieved if white space scatters the units, nor will it occur with a top-heavy or unanchored construction. There must always be the illusion of sound structural engineering—a base sturdy enough not to be upended, an axis balanced to support the appendages. Some weight, then, must anchor the layout at the base. Compare the classic architectural designs of perfectly symmetrical balance and the excitement of modern homes cantilevered over the side of a mountain, giving the occupants the thrill of being suspended in space coupled with the security of firm attachment to solid ground. Designers of such dynamic dwellings have to know all the rules of construction, all the principles of stress and balance, all the strengths and weaknesses of the materials to be used. Builders of edifices or publications must know the principles first. When they become experts, they will know when it is safe to break the rules and when it is inviting disaster. The reader may as readily be turned away by too much design as by the monotony of too much conformity.

The art of thumbnail sketching becomes a habit with the page designer who is constantly on the alert for attractive ways to display reading matter. It is not unusual to see a student editor or publications adviser stop abruptly when thumbing through a magazine, whip out a scrap of paper, and quickly sketch some interesting layout or typographical arrangement. The first rule is to work in proportion to the projected finished page. If your publication is 9 x 12 or 8 x 10 or 11½ x 14½, keep the proportion of width to height in mind when sketching a page design, or the end result will not fulfill your expectations.

Being on the lookout for graphic ideas is second nature to dedicated page designers. Most publications keep on hand an idea file of clippings and sketches of interesting page treatment, advertising

Graphics Design

layout, cover designs, and special graphics techniques that might be adapted to a particular publication's use. Just as brainstorming ideas and discussing plans with others is beneficial in expanding basic ideas into workable solutions, so using an idea file to stimulate creative design is invaluable. To establish such a file, it is a good plan to separate content into categories (covers, ads, page layout, etc.) and, when possible, include sketches showing the idea adapted to the page proportions of the publication with which you are working. A design may be electrifying in a perfect square and yet lose some of its impact when transferred to a vertical rectangular space. Something must be added or subtracted to fit the design to a new shape.

If the basic format incorporates a good balance of white space and copy, a typographical schedule that includes readable body copy; adequate spacing, sufficient variety in heading type weights and sizes, a set of stimulating standing designs (nameplates, folios, column heads, departmental identifiers, contents and calendar boxes, and the like), good photos and drawings, and appealing patterns for grouping bits of material, then the publication will find interesting pages not too difficult to achieve.

In summary, page design is a creative endeavor that opens unlimited possibilities for the makeup artist. Rather than having a set of have-to's, the few restrictions will serve best to set the beginner on course. Avoid too much excitement or too wide a variety of devices on any one spread. (In magazine design, the two facing pages are always designed as one optical unit, whether or not devoted to related material.)

1. Don't make up single pages without considering the facing page.
2. Don't lead body text unevenly; group extra white space around heads and subheads.
3. Don't crowd the space; cut the story by killing copy to assure breathing room (air).
4. Don't use too much small type in any space, especially not reverse type.
5. Don't use too many borders or other devices on the same spread, especially ads adjacent to each other.
6. Don't bump ads and pics or boxes with heavy borders.

7. Don't pyramid ads on small pages.
8. Don't group ads without text matter; a whole page of small ads will likely go unread. Advertisers deserve fair treatment, too.
9. Don't use hand-drawn borders; get type or tape for straight lines.
10. Don't use drawings or hand lettering unless a real artist is available to execute properly for reproduction.
11. Don't violate margins except with bleeds.
12. Don't forget your format specialties; include folio and departmental designators on every spread.
13. Don't copy; stretch your creative abilities to innovate.
14. Don't go overboard on variety of hand-set type; save the deviations from the standard schedule for special effect and emphasis where warranted.
15. Don't overburn or reverse on busy, patterned areas; use constant tonal gradations for readability; apply airbrushing if necessary to achieve a more even background for type.

tenure

By KAREN CROUCH

"If you're hired by a district on a permanent basis, and you complete three years of successful teaching, you can't be fired without extensive review," stated Phil Henry, RHS counselor. That, Virginia, is tenure.

Tenure is granted to a teacher after he has completed three years of satisfactory work with the district, with the approval of the principal, the superintendent, and the school board. Some people feel that tenure keeps a teacher from being fired purely because of personality conflicts with an administrator; others believe teachers tend to hide behind tenure because they know it's difficult to have them fired, while they are protected by it. Nobody, Virginia, really knows what's going on.

Is tenure hard to get, you ask? "The teacher hired has about an eight out of ten chance of getting tenure," said William F. Nance, RHS principal. "I didn't feel that it was hard for me to get it," added Mrs. Terry Alexandris, RHS teacher.

You want to know how teachers feel about tenure? "It's a protection against administrators who hire and fire on whim," said Mrs. Catherine Dunn, RHS teacher, adding, "On the other hand, if tenure were

Yes, Virginia, there are young teachers

abolished, those who are incompetent could easily be directed into other areas of employment." "I think it makes some teachers lazy," remarked Mrs. Lois Gregory, "but I think that in the first three years teachers who won't make it on the job drop out anyway. I feel that tenure is a necessary evil." You picked a goodie, Virginia. "It tends to make a lazy teacher, unless a person takes pride in his profession," stated Mrs. Alexandris. "I think it's great security for teachers, but then some people abuse it," commented Mrs. Corine Evans, adding, "In the long run I'm for tenure. I think that most people are professional enough to maintain their standards." "I guess I've never really sat down and thought about what it means to me," said Mrs. Maxine Clifford. "This year I've 'gained tenure,' but I feel no different."

Nance thinks that a contract system, limiting the number of years a teacher is hired by the district, is better than the lifetime guarantee of tenure. That way when a teacher approaches retirement age the district may retire him.

Will the tenure system ever be changed? Go away, Virginia, you ask too many questions.

Q: Many students were disappointed in last year's Makio. What have you done to obtain again?

By DAVID STOCKMAN

Many students were disappointed in last year's Makio, the yearbook. A different organizational format, duplicated photographs and irregular copy were some of the reasons for its unpopularity.

Pat Faulstich and Bob MacKimmie, this year's co-editors, are faced with the job of simply "picking up the pieces": reaffirming student belief in the Makio so they will purchase it this year, coordinating the staff which puts together this publication, and making the 1974 Makio a success.

The Makio's price this year is raised to $9.00 from the previous $7.50 it received from last year's ASB card-Makio package deal. This is because of a $1,200 debt from last year due to missing a color deadline, and the addition of several new items into this year's Makio.

The main innovation will be a spring supplement added to the book, covering many of the spring activities, such as baseball and Chepulechi items, the Makio once had to leave out because of early printing deadlines. Also, a much different cover will be seen holding the '74 book together than those covers of the past.

The Makio has always had some of the best photography in the nation. Improvements instigated by both Pat and Bob are hoped to insure a good annual.

But can Pat and Bob pull this comeback off? And what makes this year's co-editors any different from the editors of years past?

"Well, for one," Pat said, "We're the first virgins."

Makio '74: Picking up the pieces

(Top) The Hobachi, of Redlands (California) High School, in horizontal format makes a single design of one-word head, text, and breaker. White space at top frames nicely. (Bottom) Hobachi staffers demonstrate their enjoyment of headline writing, use type to carry out message of over-long kicker and demonstrate wording of actual head.

67

EQUAL RIGHTS AMENDMENT

echo editorial

skelly's blocking of era unjustified

Representative Jim Skelly, chairman of the House Commerce Committee, has single-handedly

In full, the ERA states, "Equality of rights under the law shall not be denied or abridged by the

[partial column text]

for the lower grades."
Mr. Buben would introduce calculators into the classroom after students have learned the basics of mathematics—addition, subtraction, multiplication, division, decimals and fractions. He be-

Mr. Buben shares the opinion of most of the Rincon math faculty. Student calculators should be allowed, but not recommended, in class. Ideally every student would have an identical unit for use on tests.

CALCULATORS:

A FORCE TO BE

RECKONED

WITH

Let's make a deal

Econ classes lose money in stock market

by Ed Denell

(Top) The Rincon Echo, *of Rincon High School, Tucson, Arizona, slashes type to convey message of the article.* (Middle) Echo *staffers rarely deviate from standard schedule, here for computer face to better communicate its message.* (Bottom) The Cadet Call *of Marmion Military Academy, Aurora, Illinois, simulates stock-market rise and fall for headline on graph paper, visually demonstrates story content.*

They make every day FAIR weather

By Beki Shuman
Kay Beeman

Every little boy's one-time dream is to run away and join the excitement of the fair and circus worlds. One of the few people ever to follow through with this Pinnochio life-style is Claude Jones of the Bill Haymes Show, a division of the Lubbock South-Plains Panhandle Fair.

In 1935, when he left his East Texas home while still a teenager, he joined a photo gallery and has been in the carnival business ever since—with one small exception. He gave up the fair once to manage a

By JULIE ROSENBAUM and LAURIE SHIELDS

"I would like to have the morals of a dog"

Prayers in public schools, constitutional freedoms, morals, ethics, and religion

Outspoken atheist demands freedom from religion

"Breaking like the waves"

Trouble child
Breaking like the waves at Malibu
Joni Mitchell "Court and Spark"

A student views her problems

by Linda Dryden

Even though there will always be set rules to follow, a person can do pretty much what they want to today, at least more so than ever before. Yet, just about everyone is faced with school related problems and there are different ways to solve them. Basically, a student can live with these problems or turn to someone for help, usually in some form of therapy.

Susan, a high school junior had some of the usual problems students face today and found some answers. Susan said, "School just got to be too much of a big deal. There was too much work involved to keep a happy medium. It seemed school was supposed to be my whole life. There wasn't any time to have a job, see my friends, and still keep up in school." Susan said her problems at

"I had been so good, for so long, decided to take a little pressure off," added. I started skipping school som my parents caught me. Then they (officials) looked through my recor found all the other times I had skippe this time, according to Susan, "they (administrators) didn't mak suggestions about a psychologist, but if they had my parents would have beer willing to go, at least they probably have been more open-minded.

Susan decided to see a psychologi join a therapy class. She claimed, "Bε went to therapy I though all my prc were from parents and teachers. Nov the problems that are my fault anc trying to correct these the best I can

(Top left) The Monterey Mirror *of Monterey High School, Lubbock, Texas, combines standard headline face with special-design type to convey mood.* (Right) The Anvil *of Spring Branch Memorial High School, Houston, Texas, moves headline to bottom, uses partial box to contain and attract.* (Bottom) El Gato *of Spring Branch Westchester High School, Houston, Texas, distorts type to establish thrust of story.*

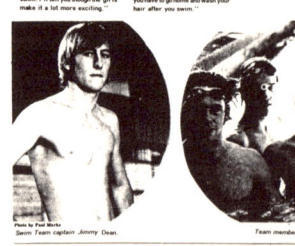

(Top) The Bugle Call *of Northeast Robert E. Lee High School, San Antonio, Texas,* uses outlined photo and movement of type to illustrate words and action in headline. (Bottom) The Anvil *uses outline letters to simulate the wording, integrates heading, photos, and text into a single design unit.*

70

The Hobachi of Redlands (California) High School, in former 11 x 7½ format (Left) shows four facets of one subject on a center spread. Symmetry is counterbalanced by varying white space, always grouped above headline in neatly mitered boxes; excitement without photos or gimmicks. (Right) Division of content on unnatural spread: air at top, full column of type separates sports briefs and feature story.

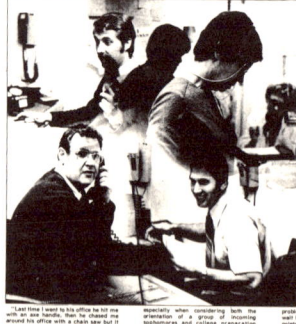

The Hobachi *of Redlands (California) High School, in 7½ x 11 format* (top) *offers exciting graphics without illustrations or fancy type. Near-perfect symmetry is broken dramatically by off-center type placement and slipped lines of head.* (Bottom) *Another center spread using composite photo and long heading anchored to body text by meeting at corner, just off-center of the middle column. Had merger of head and photo taken place over white space between columns, a division rather than a cohesion would have resulted. The Hobachi staff is long on dignity and precision with both graphics and content, yet bits of whimsy injected in each issue indicate that participants enjoy their efforts.*

72

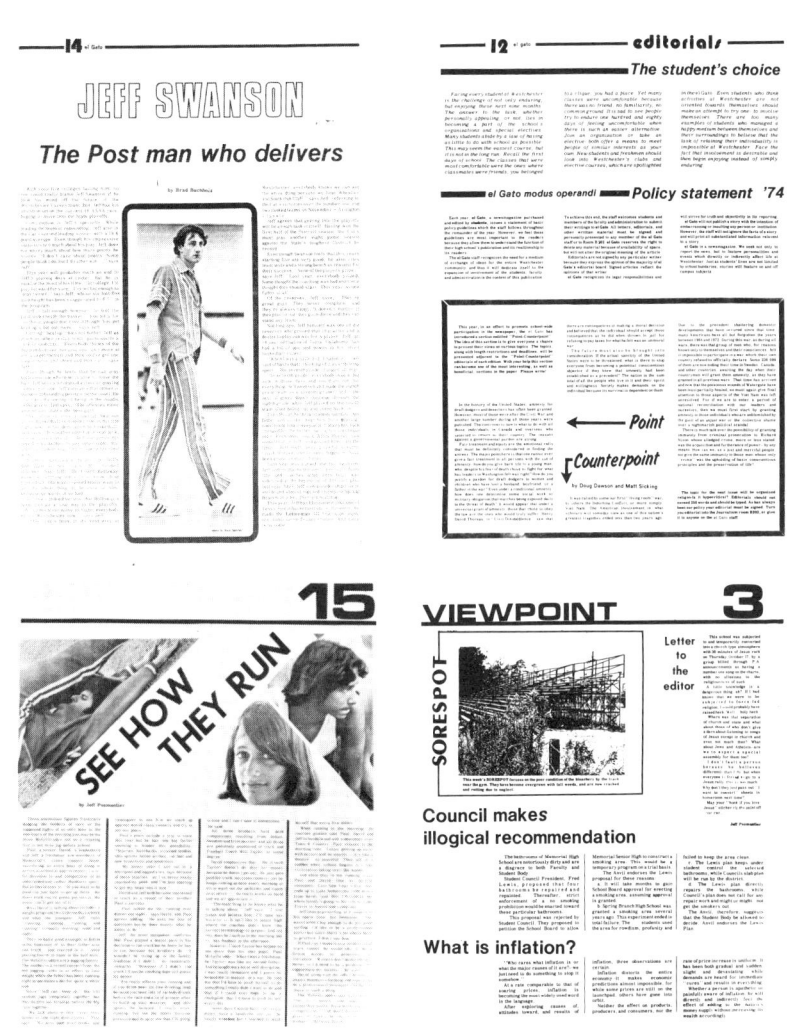

Two schools from the Spring Branch Independent School District, Houston, Texas. (Top) El Gato *of Westchester High School emphasizes height of basketball player with condensed type and tall columns, balances with horizontal head and folio line. The editorial page offers a good balance of vertical columns and horizontal rules. Right-hand headings stabilize the layout.* (Bottom) The Anvil *of Memorial High School, in new 11½ x 13¼ newsprint format, uses top two inches of pages for departmental designators and 72-pt. page numbers with dramatic impact. Creating a "track" for the headline to run in is an excellent example of visual communication. Heavy rules plus white space between columns add drama and balance. The editorial page uses white space well. Rules and box establish a focal point, provide contrast.*

The Bugle Call *of Robert E. Lee High School, San Antonio, Texas, Northeast district, was one of the top newsmagazines in the early 1970s (now one of the top full-format newspapers). This spread, unified by a 20 percent screened background, features boxed photos, heading type cut from photographs, and sufficient copy to explain the pictures and complete the message. Note folios correctly run up the left margin and down the right.*

Cover Teasers on The Cadet Call *of Marmion Military Academy, Aurora, Illinois, note key content and serve well enough as an index for the 8 to 16 pages. The 8½ x 11 newsmagazine is printed on a different color of heavy vellum each month.* (Top left) *Cover collage of bumper stickers makes room for index below nameplate.* (Top right) *Three items on inside page stand apart through use of broken box, striking bleed photo and 2-column measure for second story, and air inside border of tasteful ad.* (Wise use of extra column width in ad to balance opposite corner.) (Above) *Cover and inside page on decorated T shirts. Heading type follows simplified schedule; point size and air separate the articles.*

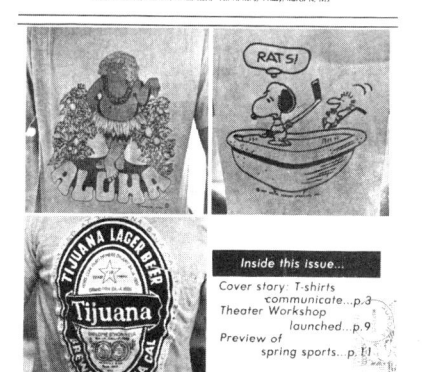

75

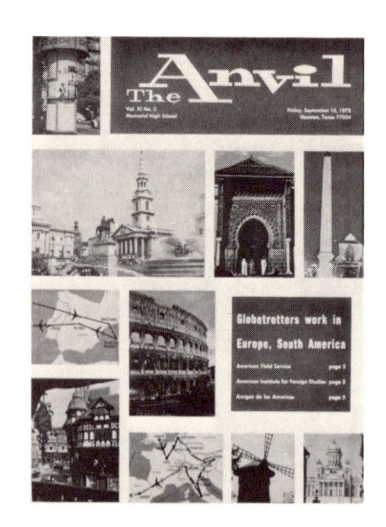

(Top life) *In the* El Gato *of Westchester High School, Spring Branch District in Houston, Texas, partly outlined photo obscures portion of logo, a solid anchor point. The vertical axis of billboard type alongside photo pulls attention to name of subject reversed on photo.* (Above right) The Anvil *of Memorial High School in the same district, features a layout from full-color travel folders reproduced in black and white. The pictures were selected for contrasts of light and dark rather than hues.* (Bottom) *Wrap-around cover carries full story for back-page feature. Entire black-and-white layout was overprinted with aqua tint block.*

76

Cover Stories in the Rincon Echo *of Rincon High School, Tucson, Arizona, are placed inside as departmentalization dictates, not always on the natural spread. A striking publication on 8½ x 11 white vellum, the* Echo *holds the top 2¾ in. of non-ad pages for numbers and departmentalizers. The shadowed typeface of the logo is repeated through these folios. Typography collage, here, artistically sets a backdrop for a historical feature on the tenth anniversary of the assassination of President John F. Kennedy. The top of the page space is used to establish mood with a drawing of an empty rocking chair and a teddy bear.* Echo *content is consistently excellent.*

VOLUME 16 • NUMBER 8 • RINCON HIGH SCHOOL • TUCSON ARIZONA 85711 • APRIL • 1974

RINCON ECHO

"You have to quit gymnastics," they said.

Injury slams door to young gymnast's athletic future

You are the best. You are number one. You have pushed your body until you knew that it could not possibly be pushed anymore. You got up and pushed it some more.

Senior Jeannette Christensen was number one. With her long blonde hair tied behind her head, she swept top girls gymnastic state and city honors for two years running. She was recognized during her first three years at Rincon as one of the top female gymnasts in Arizona. That all ended, however, when she was hurt.

Gymnastics started for Jeannette when she was eight and her mother enrolled her in a YWCA class. She enrolled Jeannette and her sisters in a combination swimming, diving and gymnastics course. Mrs. Christensen felt that her girls were watching too much television and they needed something else to do.

Jeannette soon found herself to be a natural athlete and excelled in all three sports. She also took up ballet and reveled in the freedom of ice skating.

She earned top honors in junior high school and by the time she hit Rincon, she was ready to take the state by storm. In a flurry of trophies, medals and honors she danced her way to a second place in state girls gymnastic all-around competition and then followed that with two consecutive state titles.

It was during a gymnastics invitational meet in Reno, Nevada during May 1973 that she noticed her back was hurting. The pain wasn't bad, just a dull ache, but if she arched her back, little darts of pain would shoot up her spine.

At the time, she was practicing from three to four, sometimes even five, hours a day after school. Once in a while she would go to the YWCA for two more hours of extra work.

Throughout diving season the pain increased steadily and hampered her in her meets.

"It just kept getting worse," she says, "It wouldn't go away."

Finally, after a particularly painful meet in Texas she went to see a doctor. She went to see several doctors. They all told her the same thing.

"You have to quit gymnastics, they said. If she didn't, by the time she turned 25 she might need a spinal fusion. Two of the vertebra in her back were touching.

"I couldn't believe it," says Jeannette's sister Karen, a Rincon sophomore, "I just couldn't believe it. It seemed like Jeannette was always in gymnastics and always would be. I remember my mother went with Jeannette to the doctors and when they got back, they were both crying."

Jeannette demonstrates the ability that led her to two straight all-around state titles. Although she can no longer compete, she is dedicated to helping her teammates.

Jeannette admits to being very upset and crying over her disappointment for the following two days.

"All that work," she sighs. But I finally faced up to it. I realized that there were more things to life than gymnastics and diving." Besides being in sports, Jeannette is a member of the National Honor Society and plays the flute in the band.

She reduced her gymnastics practice to almost nothing although she spent considerable time helping the rest of the team. She was unanimously elected captain by the team at the beginning of the year and her sister Karen was elected co-captain.

The girls' gymnastic coach, Miss Marcia Champlin, says, "Jeannette is an excellent coach and teacher. Even with her back problem she is very much a part of the team. She is a natural leader."

The team needed her to compete against Santa Rita in the home opener, March 12. She agreed to do a compulsory routine on the balance beam. A compulsory routine is a certain set of gymnastic movements every gymnast must perform alike. "A compulsory won't hurt me," she said.

The gym was dead silent as Jeannette dipped and rolled and danced on the beam. Her body moved with a practiced grace and she appeared sure of herself. She smiled.

When she dismounted with no sign of serious trouble, the crowd went wild. Her teammates rushed out to slap her on the back and hug her. They gave her a several-minute standing ovation.

"I guess I compete because I'm basically a competitor. Maybe it's just a feeling of accomplishment when I do something right.

Maybe that's it. Or maybe it's just stubborn pride.

Whatever it is, Jeannette Christensen gets results. She's number one!

By Rusty Greene

THAT'S PAR

A word about our jock doc

After discovering who keeps the purple machine healthy, I can't resist some jock talk about the jock doc and his chalk talk.

The University of Arizona sponsors the Athletic Training Internship Program for Tucson High Schools. Through this program, Rincon was fortunate enough to receive Mr. Dave Knoeppel, 25, as its head athletic trainer.

Mr. Knoeppel is a part-time trainer and part-time student of the UofA. He holds a Bachelor of Science degree and is aiming for his Master of Science, which he expects to complete this August.

Despite conducting an apparently monotonous routine of taping and wrapping, Mr. Knoeppel finds his job challenging.

"I enjoy the work here," he says. "I've never considered it a boring job. The atmosphere that is produced through the interaction of myself and the people I train has a tendency to reduce the boredom of the tasks that I do." Translated into English, he enjoys the company of his athletic patients.

The feeling is mutual.

Steve Andre

Rincon Echo *staffers not only write and design content, but they can set type and have mastered the art of following the contour of illustrations. The Consistency of headline faces throughout the publication balances this body text accent as well as the high design of folio face. Here rhythm and movement are created by repetition of single image eight times; quotation aligned with logo establishes vertical axis to provide stability. Division of the two articles on the inside spread is accomplished easily by the direction of outlined photo and the location of departmentalizer and cartoon over the second story.*

78

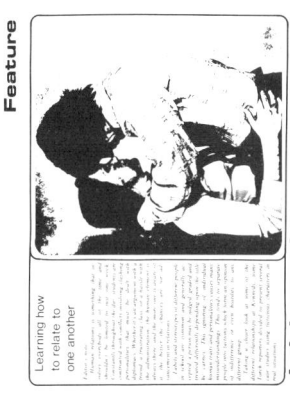

The Torch of John F. Kennedy High School, Bloomington, Minnesota, is an excellent 8½ x 11 newsmagazine on offset vellum. Published monthly, The Torch uses a subdued billboard technique on each cover as a sufficient index, spotlighting major content including cover story. A staff of writers diligently examines various facets of the cover story. Here, the spread on relating is unified by horizontal heads in the same typeface. Contrast is achieved in photo treatment and the vertical arrangement of the smaller pictures.

The Torch, Kennedy High School, Bloomington, Minn., uses humor in photo composition for this cover story on the money crunch. Inside spread is a study in rhythms and contrast. Horizontal head unifies the layout, vertical column dividers rhythmically separate, yet connect, the content. Repeat pattern for photos and heading type also add cohesion. A pleasing, easy-to-read arrangement which does not need the natural fold. The care exhibited in planning cover photo and page design is also evident in the quality of the writing.

Cover Stories in West Side Story of West High School, Iowa City, Iowa, are located on the center spread. When only eight pages, WSS may run articles on page one. Here logo placement allows room for two stories and lively illustration plus index notation, all aided by a unifying border. The spread offers four more stories on entertainment theme. Rhythmic repetition of bold column rules balances violent movement of 218-pt. head and strong silhouettes. WSS uses Helvetica head schedule except for special displays. Visual excellence is backed with quality copy.

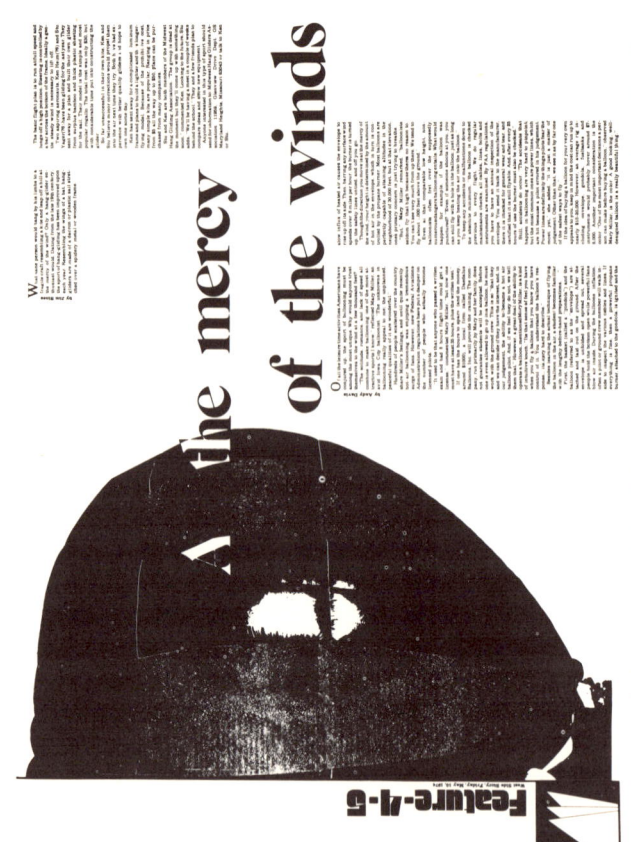

West Side Story of Iowa City, Iowa, is a dramatic magazine at 11½ x 17. With large pages, WSS uses white space lavishly. Folio and departmentalizers run vertically in 2-inch outside margin on left-hand pages above distinctive logo. This cover and spread were printed in yellow and black. Yellow was used for 24-pt. initials beginning each article. Heading type reverses over dark areas of photo. Text, placed for balance, not column structure, defines top and right margins, establishes an "airborne" feeling for the layout.

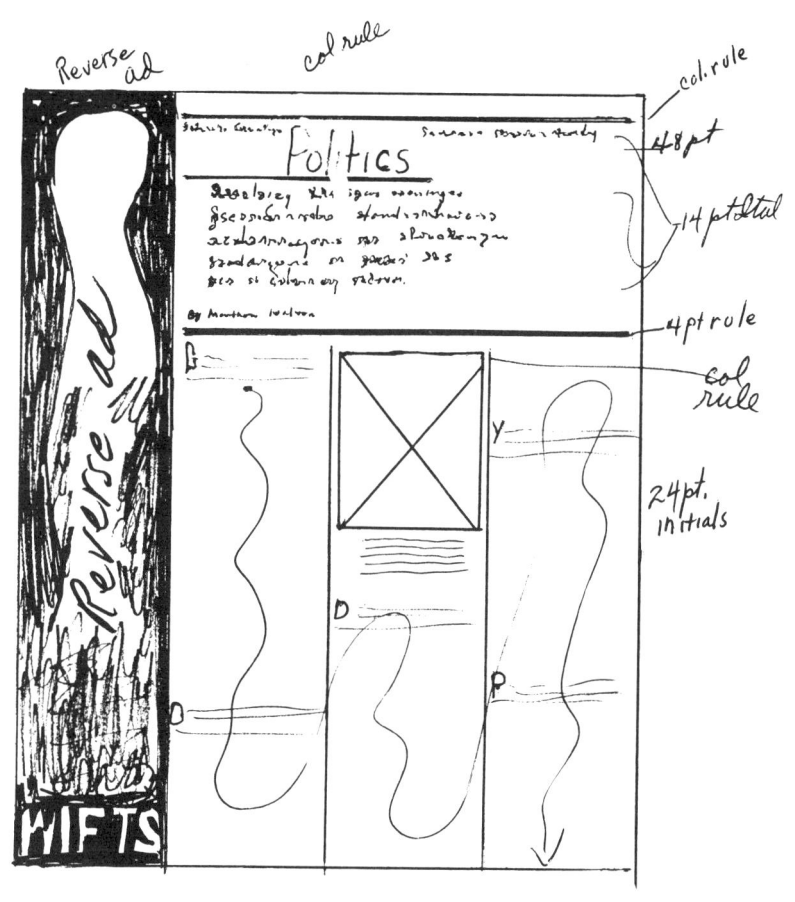

Sketch Dummy of a 4-column page with 1 column reverse ad and 3 columns of text. The heading, 6 lines of 14-point type accented with a short line of 48-point, is boxed with column rule on top and 4-point rule (could be a thick and thin line combination) at the bottom. Initials in 24 points are scattered through the text for a visual surprise. The small illustration and its cutline are dropped in over the center column. Horizontal rules and lines of head contrast with the vertical force of black ad. Small pic adds needed weight in center and balance by its proximity to headline box. Had picture run at the end of the text, it would have appeared too detached; in the right-hand column, it would have formed a hangman's noose and detracted from the reading.

Rough Sketch for 2-column ad on 5-column page. Three columns left for the text are portioned off by a 4-point black rule which forms a rounded corner, three-sided box for a side-bar feature or statistical material that relates to major article. Copy for the article is set at 2 columns, dropping to 1½ adjacent to box. Heading uses two lines of 14-point type flanking a single 48-point line, set off by column rules from departmental or column title and the text. By-line over text aligns with head.

The Shield, *McCallum High School, Austin, Texas,* achieves harmony in typography and in display of ads and text matter. Excitement is added with dramatic photos and the technique of dropping related photos on dead areas of a single background picture. Bold face lead-ins provide visual impact in long columns of type.

85

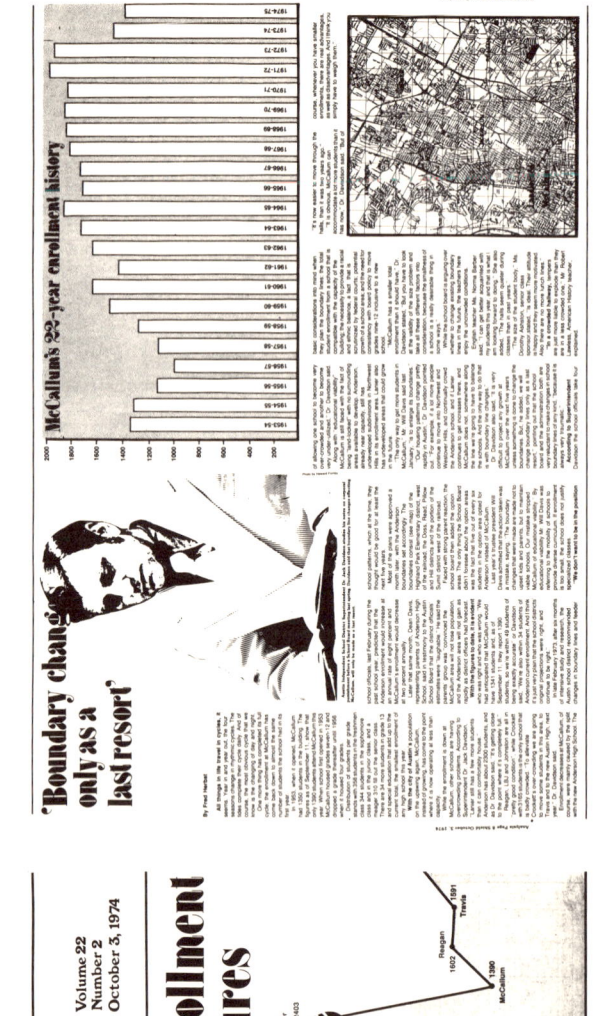

Outstanding graphic design is characteristic of The Shield. Here mood type combines with an attractive graph to set the stage for the lead story. On the center spread, the display incorporates a partially outlined high contrast photo, a screened chart, and a map to amplify the text. Note bold face lead-ins, outside margin complete folios, and the unifying design element of narrow rules, top and bottom, on all pages.

Chapter IV

PHOTOGRAPHIC ILLUSTRATIONS

One of the greatest single improvements in the appearance of printed periodicals over the centuries has been that of photographic illustrations. Not even color adds as much to reader interest. Photojournalism is a separate career. The photojournalist's job, like the reporter's, is to communicate information. And, just as the reporter has refined the task to strive for more complete and compelling reporting, so the news photographer strives for as much substance as possible in the picture and adds an artistic approach to the composition. Many newspaper pages of yesteryear were adorned with "check passing" pictures wherein the recipient of an award accepted the token from a representative of the endowing agency. Other photos clichés often seen were of persons holding plaques or trophies close to the ear in order to get both face and the award in a 1-column by 2-in. space. Old-time photographers were schooled to tell as much of the story as possible with the camera lens, to pose the subjects in front of or holding "identifiers" that set the scene or showed the reason for the photograph. Establishing the setting and identifying the reason for the picture are still necessary, but modern photographers have learned to incorporate artistic appreciation of form, thereby doubling the reader's interest in the resulting photograph. Composition and content work together to achieve maximum impact with each photograph. Magazine readers expect both information and enjoyment from the illustrations in a publication.

PHOTOS IN PAGE DESIGN

The role of the photograph in page design is a significant one. In magazine journalism, the pictures are relied upon to attract attention, help lure the reader into the story, and carry a significant portion of the communication burden—both informational and emotional. The first rule in placing photographs on the page should be "THINK BIG!" Even though newsmagazine pages are usually smaller than newspaper pages, photographic images must not shrink proportionately. The old rule of "no face smaller than the size of a dime" really should be inflated to the size of a quarter or preferably a 50-cent piece. Small pages with minuscule photographs are as dull as unbroken gray columns. That space would be better used in relief —for openness around the display type—than crammed with pictures too small for easy recognition. The second rule should call for technical excellence: focus and contrast. These are responsibilities of the photographer, true, and both picture taker and picture printer should exert every effort to achieve perfection in both areas. The persons in charge of making up the pages may be at the mercy of those technicians and find themselves faced with using weak prints or none at all. Unless the content of the photograph is of such importance that quality is secondary (as when a famous person has appeared on campus, a building has burned down, or the photographer has caught the rivals in the act of stealing the school mascot), the preferred option would be to omit the photo. The editorial staff and the photographers should agree that only top-quality prints will be accepted for reproduction.

Makeup artists need to learn not only what makes a technically excellent photograph, but what makes a good picture in order to achieve the best effect from photos in their publication. What makes a good picture brings up rule three: strive for interesting composition. Just as writers are continually told to use the active voice, not the passive, and to employ explicit descriptions to achieve colorful language, so the persons involved with photographs should avoid static groupings—rows of people lined up as if for a firing squad—and confusing backgrounds that detract from the clarity of the message. Action shots have more interesting stories to tell, and even pictures of two people are more appealing if the shutter is snapped while they are informally chatting rather than both facing the camera saying "cheese." Candid or casual shots that catch the subjects in natural expressions add life and vitality to the stories they accompany. Such pictures take little more time to accomplish than posed "mug" shots.

Newsmagazines do not absolutely need pictorial matter to relieve the gray pages; many other graphic devices are available. Photographs, however, can add greatly to reader interest if they themselves are interesting. People like to see good pictures. They like to see pictures of their friends and of important people. They even like to see pictures of places and events with which they are familiar. They do not, however, like to strain their eyes to identify tiny faces or to figure out the action in a small, muddy photograph. Pictures should add drama and interest to a page, not pose more work for the reader.

Composition goes beyond including action or informality in a photograph. Background and foreground are important to the clarity and the visual impact. Backgrounds should never detract from or interfere with the focal point. Pictures of people in front of hedges or trees often give the impression that green things are growing out of the person. A refuse can or unsightly utility post can dominate a picture through contrast with the other elements. Attractive objects in the foreground such as a tree branch or building arch, on the other hand, can serve to enhance the composition by framing the focal point and controlling the overall pattern. Just as perfect symmetry is rejected by page artists as too static and too dull, asymmetrical balance in photographic images adds drama, depth, and distinction. Never have the focal point in dead center, vertically or horizontally. For a more pleasing apportionment of the space, divide it into thirds in both directions and concentrate subject matter where these imaginary lines intersect. A significant difference between a snapshot and a photograph is that intangible composition quality known as depth of field. Whereas snapshots often focus on the subject squarely in the center of the area, good composition often "frames" the subject with some object in the foreground that defines the contour, yet focuses on the subject near the middle of the field of perspective but off-center in the two-dimensional plane of the finished print.

Cropping for Composition

Perfect composition does not always happen on the negative. Many photographers print only a portion of the film frame to sharpen the composition by eliminating unnecessary or unwanted areas. Persons working with pictures to be reproduced in publications need to learn how to crop away the unwanted portions of a photographic print to concentrate on the "picture." Cropping away outside areas enlarges the image and brings the attention to the exact part of the photo to be emphasized. Remember, the space allotted for a photograph on the newsmagazine page is to be generous, preferably one column in width for each person in the picture. A one-column photo of a person that includes the entire head with a quarter-inch background on either side will be large enough to be interesting; yet, if the same picture is cropped at the ear nearest the camera and the remaining portion of the face is enlarged to fill the same one-column space, the picture will appear to be about one-fourth larger; it will be electrifyingly attention-getting. The impact will be far greater than the full-head shot and well worth the "loss" of the ear. A two-column reproduction of the 25-member football squad will not have the interest, even for the team, than one action shot of an end-around play or spectacular tackle will have. To the average reader, one game shot looks much like the next. Only by dramatic enlargement and strategic cropping of a technically good picture can the action of a sport really be transmitted to the printed page.

Learning to crop and proportion pictures for reproduction is as necessary to the page designer as knowing typographic characteristics and limitations. Cropping is finding the "composition" in the photographic print, eliminating the unwanted or unnecessary areas. Cropping is always done by paring the photographic image from the outside edge to some line parallel to that edge, figuratively. Some photos can be improved by cropping on all four sides, not necessarily by the same amounts; some may need trimming on only one edge. Some may be printed crooked and need alignment of the edges with the natural uprights of gravitational force. After cropping, the picture may be a different shape—wider or higher—than the piece of paper on which it is printed, but the image to be reproduced should still have four 90-degree angles; it should be a perfect rectangle. The portion to be cropped away may be indicated on the surface of the print by marking in the white margin with yellow grease pencil, making extensions of the horizontal and vertical edges of the portion to be reproduced. Or the crop marks may be made lightly on the back of the photographic print in very soft pencil, showing the rectangle of the desired picture.

SCALING FOR REPRODUCTION

Figuring reduction or enlargement, that is, proportioning this cropped image to the space it will occupy on the printed page involves some form of mathematical exercise. Proportion wheels are easy to master, and directions for use are usually printed on them. Proportion wheels are pairs of cardboard discs mounted one upon the other and scored much like a slide rule to indicate relative measurements (the original against the projected, or height against width) for any reduction or enlargement. What this exemplifies is that the proportion (or relationship) of the height to the width never changes, whether reducing or enlarging the picture. If a photo is 6 in. wide and 4 in. high on the finished print (cropped portion) it will be 3 to 2 no matter if it is enlarged to 8 in. wide (by 5⅓ high) or reduced to 4 in. wide (by 2⅔ high). Elaborate cropping L's are available that can be manipulated to block away portions of a photograph to help decide which is the most dramatic portion to reproduce and, at the same time, offer scaling information as provided by the proportion wheels. Both wheels and L's cost some money but do offer speedy and fairly accurate calculations as to the final specifications for a picture on the printed page. They provide a method for determining how much space a picture will occupy, and they can be "turned around" to indicate where a photo must be cropped if the allotted space on the page is so locked-in that flexibility in shape or size is not permitted, and the picture must be manipulated rather than the space.

There are two other methods for determining the proportions of the final image, and these require no equipment except a ruler. Algebraically, the formula is: **a** (original width) is to **b** (original height) as **x** (projected width) is to **y** (projected height). When one of the projected dimensions is known, the other can be determined. Often the column measure is the factor that sets the width limitation of the reproduced image. That figure compared to the original width yields the percentage of the original height that the projected height will be.

This formula illustrated geometrically is the easiest to visualize and gives the most accurate appraisal of dimensions of the projected image. Using right angles of a corner of a blank sheet of paper, draw a rectangle the exact size (or to exact scale) of the cropped photographic image. Then draw a diagonal line from one corner of the rectangle to the opposite corner, extending the line beyond the original points if the picture is to be enlarged. When either of the final measurements (the width or height) that the picture is to be on the printed page is determined, then measure that amount on the side of the rectangle to which it corresponds. If the print is 6 in. high and is to be enlarged to 8, measure along each vertical side of the rectangle 2 in. beyond the 6 of the original diagram, and draw a horizontal line connecting these two points, continuing it until it meets the diagonal line. The length of this horizontal line will be the projected width of the reproduction. Dimensions for any reduction or enlargement of the original shape are set at any point along that diagonal where a horizontal and a vertical line intersect. The diagonal insures that the width will maintain the same proportion to the height as in the original picture. As with the wheel, if the final space allotment is predetermined and inflexible, the reverse of the above procedure will indicate the proportions to which the original photo must be cropped.

Techniques for Special Effects

In addition to strategic cropping, drama can be injected into photographs through special graphic techniques. Gimmicks will not save an inherently bad photograph, but some special effects can intensify the drama or give a strong assist in projecting an emotion. Sometimes a photo somewhat weak in contrast can be intensified through use of posterization or the duotone process in which two images are made and printed on top of each other. These are somewhat costly, because they require two runs through the press, but they can be worth it when the content of the picture warrants. There are screens that can add unusual textures to the print image: concentric circles overlaid on a picture tend to project action even from a passive subject; different patterns such as mezzotint or steel engraving can create some special feeling; enlarged dots project modern technological influences. Ghosting the image, to make it weaker, by asking the photolithographer to "screen" it out to 20 percent or 30 percent of normal reproduction intensity is sometimes used with or behind type to indicate an activity or set a tone. Ghosting for overprinting should be done only with pictures that are near monotone in composition. Printing over a photograph will make the type more difficult to read, and if the photograph has a strong light-and-dark interchange, the type will fade into the dark areas and send the reader to the next page. If there is much variance in the tonal qualities of a picture, it is best to surprint in a solid area, such as the sky, or to mortise an unimportant portion (blank out a specified area much like placing a piece of white paper over the spot) and drop the printing in that space. Reversing the surprinted type in a dark area or in a black mortise can be dramatic. Printers can help by using an airbrush to make the area to be surprinted more uniform in tonal range.

Offset printing involves the photographing of the finished pages and combining screened halftones with the line negatives of pure black and white type and drawings. The photolithographer can add some sparkle during the process of making the screened negative. At this time patterned screens can be added, or the picture shot without screening of any kind to convert a halftone photograph into a line shot resembling an ink drawing. This is called an art conversion in photolithography, and the unschooled eye cannot tell the difference between an art conversion in the lithographer's camera and a "high contrast" print from the photographer's darkroom in which a contrasty negative is printed on extra contrast paper to block out the gradations and produce a primarily black-and-white-only print. Such converted pictures add stark drama to the printed page. Naturally, this technique is not suitable for pictures whose subject matter should be depicted in detail, but rather is to be reserved for those arty or mood shots where the image is meant to represent a myriad of persons or situations. Such photos lend additional impact to articles about sociological problems such as drug abuse, vandalism, or job opportunities. Often the image in the picture is outlined, with the background either dropped out by the photolithographer or blocked out by the graphic artist. Combination pictures with some of the image outlined and the balance intact to complete the portion of the rectangle make the better choice. Photographs appear most often on the printed page as unadorned blocks, screened or dotted to project the image. When thin black lines are added to define the perimeter of the picture, the effect is sharpened.

Whether special effects are employed or photos are printed "straight," their contribution to the effectiveness of the page is influenced by (*1*) the size of the image, (*2*) the quality of the photograph itself, (*3*) the interest generated by the composition, and (*4*) the artistic aspects of the photo's integration with the overall design. Addition of special effects cannot compensate for weaknesses in these fundamentals, but they can enhance the total effectiveness.

PHOTOS AS FEATURES

Occasionally a photograph conveys the major portion of a message and serves as the primary communicator with only a caption to add those details no picture can record—date, names, scene of action, and significance or implication. Called photo stories or features, such single-picture features may be boxed and the cutline, which probably will run longer than a standard caption, should have some kind of large type heading such as a catchline or headline between the picture and the "copy." Sideheads, set-in headings, or headline-type beginnings that read into the body of the cutline may be used. Publications staffs that plan to run photo features with any frequency should settle on one effective style of display for borders and headings and stick with it, incorporating it into the structural format and typographical schedule. The practice of presenting certain kinds of material on a recurring basis with consistency of display builds that familiarity with the format which establishes reader association.

When more than a single picture is needed to communicate a story adequately and a photo layout is desired, the principles of page design must be brought into use. That all-important white space plays a significant role in framing and connecting the pieces. Whereas numerous lines of body type need the repetition of column width to hold them together, separate photographs in a grouping may serve the layout better if their sizes and shapes vary, when the pictures are of such size in themselves as to be able to stand alone. The old yearbook layout rule of employing different shapes and sizes of rectangles with one dominant element, either larger or heavier, as a

Photographic Illustrations

focal point can be adapted for the photo essay. However, more interesting designs are open to the newsmagazine, because here the photo feature is a one-time composition and the designer need not be concerned with preceding or succeeding page layouts. Whether some of the special effects discussed previously are included or not, the entire grouping will be enhanced if bordered in some way. And there must be some large heading type, arranged as a unit, not scattered about over the page. Cutlines are necessary to identify every person and the action in each photo. These may be clustered with identifiers preceding each caption within the block, such as "top left, center, lower left, lower right, opposite page"; or they may run under, over, or beside each individual picture, but they *must* be there to complete the recording of the message. It is usually necessary to add several short paragraphs of text in addition to the cutlines, explaining the scene and the action and giving the reader the background and the reason the photographic coverage is presented. Homecoming activities, school dramatic productions, or carnivals often call for such treatment because the activities hold interest for a large segment of the readership, yet little copy can be written to capture the events as graphically as the camera can. Not only will the type block complete the informational message, but the contrast in texture will complement the layout. White space should not appear in large portions within the layout, but it will serve to unify the design if kept basically to the outside. The addition of that border frame will help to force the various pieces together. If bleed photos are used, they can fracture the border without detracting from its effectiveness; the contrast can add another plus to the design.

Photomontages, or photographic collages in which numerous photos are cut or torn in odd shapes and arranged to form a single "picture," call for an artist's touch. Neatness is important in the effectiveness of a collage. Frayed edges, sharp and uncontoured outlines, and pieces with so little contrast that they run together, all detract from the effect. Photographs can be torn with the back side forced away from the tear to avoid a white edge. Less rigid printed pieces can be successfully trimmed by nimble fingers to follow the contours of the object and eliminate the background. Sharp-bladed artist's knives produce a crisp edge, especially for straight lines; and water-based paints or photo retouch solutions can be used to clean up distracting areas of separate pieces or the finished whole. Collective pictures should be arranged along the same principles of balance, contrast, and concord as called for in a page design.

CUTLINES FOR CLARITY

Every picture, including those used on the cover, must have a caption or a cutline. The reader is entitled to know why an illustration is included, the identity of the person(s) in the photograph, the setting, the occasion, the day, and any significant or related facts not obvious in the photograph. Even the chief administrator of the school needs identification; there may be some newcomers or outsiders who do not know the identity of even celebrities, and documentation for the permanent record is part of the object in reporting. Few people will remember names to fit the faces in future years.

Cutline writing has as many clichés as photojournalism. It is not necessary to say "pictured above . . ." because that should be obvious. "Left to right" is so well established as the standard pattern that only when the direction is some other arrangement such as clockwise or from the top is there a need to instruct the reader's eye. Faked "candid" shots of old usually attributed some action to the major subject in a picture while the others named "looked on." If contrived photos can be avoided, this outmoded practice can be buried. If the photographer can catch the real action, the cutline writer can complete the message with the same vitality, describing the part of the scene not explained by the camera, identifying the persons and their actions or the reasons for same, and giving the reader full satisfaction.

The positioning of cutlines and the typographical design depend on the format specifications. Type should not be identical to body type. Cutlines may be set slightly larger or smaller, in italics (though not the best choice), or boldface. They may be set unjustified if body copy is set justified, or vice versa, flush left, or flush right for contrast. Placement is not by a set rule; it may vary with page design. Although cutlines should be set the same way throughout a publication, placement can be fitted to best complement the layout. On standard inside pages, consistency of caption placement will be pleasing to the reader, but on special design pages, some deviation will be acceptable. For photo essays involving groups of illustrations, cutlines may be clustered for design purposes, so long as there is easy identification between picture and explanation. One to one will remain the more readable arrangement for photos and cutlines. Sometimes a layout may call for the cutline to run beside a picture, or above a bottom bleed, or right on the photo itself. So long as typography is consistent, the reader will readily accept a shift in placement. Cutlines are better typographically if they have some large-type intro, perhaps a sidehead or an all-caps lead-in, especially if captions are set in standard-weight type. Boldface typography does a better job of carrying cutlines without the aid of display type than does standard. If no display type is planned except on special photo features, captions should be written as concisely as possible to keep them short. When captions are to follow the column width of the photos they accompany, they should be set two picas shorter (one pica indentation on each side in the column). Cutlines in magazine journalism can be more dramatic if set at a narrower measure and positioned under one side or the other of the photo, using the resulting blank space to set them off, rather than display type. Or they may be placed beside the picture, aligned with top or bottom lateral. What really matters is that they be included, and that they function.

Each photograph should also be accompanied by a credit line identifying the photographer. Professional publications take as much pride in their photojournalists' work as in that of their reporters. Often they identify their photographers as staffers in the credit lines, as "Gazette photo by G. A. Zette." The credit line can be the last line in a cutline, set off by parentheses. It may be set in smaller type than that used for either cutlines or body copy, boldface, standard, or even italics. It may be run between cutline and picture, over the cut, up the side, or even surprinted or reversed inside the picture area. When several pictures by the same photographer are used, a separate credit line similar to the by-line should be included in the page layout, omitting the single picture credits. This photo credit line may be set slightly smaller than the reporter's by-line and placed elsewhere in the layout, or it may be in the same type and immediately under the by-line. When cluster captions are used, it is acceptable to identify the photographers in that copy and omit the other credit lines. The staff should weigh the contribution the photographer's work makes and give full credit where it is due.

Summarizing, the staffers setting out to enhance their publication with photographic illustrations must strive for quality in three areas: technical excellence, compositional artistry and communication, and cutline amplification. As individuals on a team, they will concentrate on:

1. Creative ways to communicate the message through photography, avoiding dull and trite composition.
2. Technical excellence in film exposure, development, and printing.
3. Bold treatment in incorporating the photographic image into the layout, calling for dramatic cropping, large space allotment, and creative arrangement with other elements in the design.
4. Special effects only when their use is warranted by the importance of the text material, not resorting to use of gimmickry for the sake of gimmickry and destroying much of the impact through overuse.
5. Well-written cutlines for every photo to amplify the message, telling what the reader needs to know that the photographs cannot tell completely.
6. Consistency of typography for cutlines and photo credits.

Chapter V

THE ALL-IMPORTANT CONTENT

Striking visual appeal is only half the reason newsmagazine journalism is popular with both staffs and readers. The shift in approach to content means more exercise in writing skills and a wider range of topics. The format appeals because it fosters emphasis on subject matter that has greater impact on the reader.

Clearing the pages of the clutter of small news items opens space for longer articles that offer edification or entertainment, copy that relates to existing interests of the readers.

CONTENT CLASSIFICATION

Kinds of content consistent with newsmagazine format may appear to follow the same categories found in school newspapers. However, it is not just an increase in feature material that distinguishes the magazine. The approach to content must be different or the effect is lost. News stories of limited significance should be collected and displayed in a column for spot-news briefs. Some accounts will be longer than others; this will offer the contrast needed to achieve an interesting layout.

Spot-news events of considerable importance, such as the all-school carnival or drama production, warrant more display. Such events, often handled as advance stories to increase attendance, call for news feature treatment. To help generate interest, the descriptive phrases and colorful language of feature writing are appropriate. Background material adds emphasis, anecdotes increase interest, and a snappy writing style lends an aura of excitement. Featurizing should be reserved for larger news stories that are noncontroversial, do not deal with serious problems, and are on subjects suited to such lighthearted treatment. Some ongoing news stories, such as controversies over traffic problems near the school or a campaign to raise funds for a new gymnasium, lend themselves to interpretation or explanation of the situations. New school board rulings or state laws may need analysis of what they may mean to students and their pursuits. The use readers will make of the information will influence choice of writing style.

Factual accounts in newsmagazines tend to concentrate on the why and the how elements in the news more than the other four W's. Who, what, when, and where become supportive facts in the in-depth articles. In-depth reports, interpretive articles, news analyses, and a variety of subjective commentaries referred to loosely as advocacy journalism or the "new journalism," are types of newsmagazine writing in which the reporter must dig beyond the immediate event to complete the picture.

Reporting in depth involves first concentrating on the background of a news event, telling the circumstances or conditions that brought it about, then showing the relationship of one segment of the news to other areas of current involvement. It means objective reporting that goes deeper than the surface but sticks to the facts and allows the reader to decide what use is to be made of the information.

Interpretive articles involve explanation or speculation on the meaning or significance of events in terms of causes and effects. This is a somewhat more subjective treatment of the news, such as the television news commentator might employ. Interpretive articles deal with the facts and background of a news item and the possible consequences of connecting links to other events. Reporters assigned to such articles must be knowledgeable in the field of the discussion, or should seek interpretation from authoritative sources in the particular area. Whenever sources other than the reporter are quoted, verbatim or in summary, their names and identifications should appear in the story, even if the quotes are from previous publications.

Analyzing the news and interpreting its meaning or significance is like diagnosis and prognosis. A measure of subjectivity enters in the approach of the examiner, but news analysts and interpreters are expected to strive for objectivity in examination under the high standards of ethical journalism. Analyzing the news implies attempting to examine a situation from all points of view and explain what it means to each segment, projecting possible reverberations of future circumstances in light of current information. Here again, student reporters may need to seek more experienced authorities in the areas under analysis to avoid shortsighted interpretation.

Advocacy communication is considerably more personal in approach. Articles deliberately directed at persuading readers to embrace a specific point of view should be clearly labeled as opinion of the writer. Readers like to discover how different authorities react to particular news situations. They habitually seek out the writings of well-known columnists in periodicals. However, readers demand credibility. They expect advocates to have experience and extensive knowledge in areas in which they offer advice or admonitions. Journalists who become effective advocates are usually well known first as thorough reporters. It is frequently from a long-term assignment on one specific beat that a specialization develops to provide this depth of knowledge and expertise.

The "new journalism" strays into a somewhat fictionalized or narrative approach to reporting. Some call it humanistic. It is the antithesis of the reporter's being "only the instrument of communication," with absolute objectivity in writing style. "New" journalists recount events with reporter and reader involvement, reacting and interacting with the people and developments in a news event, a sort of "We were there" approach. This kind of writing, often employing the literary devices and style associated with narrative, is suited to personal-account features of adventure or triumph over obstacles for the school publication. If use of first-person articles could be saved for such suspense and drama stories, the style would be effective and offer contrast. Use of the first person in too many stories gives a publication the appearance of detachment from the audience; it indicates that staff members are more concerned with their roles as writers than with the readers' part as an active audience. When a journalist is recounting someone else's adventure, the focus should be on the adventurer, and the third person is the more effective narrative form.

Personality profiles involve a bit of all the above activities in investigative reporting, plus a special knack for interviewing. To capture someone's personality on paper requires skill in asking questions, in listening, in observing unsaid things, and in remembering. The writer must be able to recreate the circumstance, setting, tone and feeling, and incidental actions as well as the appearance and statements of the interviewee. Considerable preparation is required before the interview—gathering information on the background and accomplishments of the person. Skill is required at asking the right questions, hearing the "whole" answer, and having the mental agility to follow a different tack if some unexpected bit of information indicates a new area to pursue. And, naturally, the interviewer must have considerable facility with the language and writing skills to recreate on paper the dynamism of a personality.

The longer articles characteristic of newsmagazines may fall into the above categories. They may also run the gamut of feature-writing styles and subjects—explanatory features, historical or seasonal features, how-to articles, stories on leisure pursuits, and humorous or literary writings, among others.

Departmentalization

Division of content usually dictates departments for news, special investigative articles, sports, entertainment features, opinion and comment, and often a people section. These areas can be subdivided within the groupings; they can be eliminated or others added. Content and what it is called will vary with the individual publication and the emphasis each espouses. Labeling can be as general as the broad designations of news, sports, features, and opinion, but more imaginative titles set a livelier stage. Active, descriptive expressions help draw readers to the articles. "News Focus" or "News Scope" indicate that some sharpening of the reporting has been done; "Action" indicates lively encounters; "Spotlight" or "Close Up" tell the reader that "Here is the featured act." "Forum," "Viewpoint," "Input," "Voices," "Feedback," or "Speaking Out" are more inviting titles than Editorials or Opinion. "Sights and Sounds" or "Steppin' Out" suggest entertainment or leisure content. "Que Passe?" and "Around the School" have more going for them than News Briefs. Variations on the school name or mascot may dictate some standing column head or department nomenclature. Freed-Hardeman College, in Henderson, Tennessee, has a distinctive signature cut (or logo) involving the initials F.H.; the newspaper, *Bell Tower,* uses this logo at the top of its calendar of coming events with the words Future Happenings for a play on the familiar letters.

The philosophy of the publication dictates somewhat the variety of departments, the emphasis for each, and the sequence. Newsmagazines concentrating on strong leadership in guiding students' actions may well lead off with opinion pages. Those attempting to reach a broad spectrum of the general audience may emphasize news and related factual matter in the opening section. The primarily feature magazines are likely to play up such material first. To reap the special display advantages of the broad center spread, some staffs prefer to use the middle of the publication for their major thrust. Each staff must make the decisions as to sequence in light of its own aims and attitudes.

Whatever the sequence, content is divided and grouped under departmental labels and should follow the same order in each standard issue. For special editions built on particular themes, deviations from the norm should be self-explanatory, but readers generally appreciate a regular sequence in the arrangement of sections.

CONTENT APPORTIONMENT

Each division of subject matter should be watched for balance of coverage. In news departments, every effort should be exerted to include curriculum and community coverage as well as student activities and social affairs. As many phases of the curriculum as possible should receive attention through the year even though spot news copy may flow more readily from certain areas. Likewise with sports, not all the space should be devoted to major sports and varsity teams at the expense of "B" teams, girls' sports, and athletic competitions that attract fewer spectators. Each segment of the school or reader-related activity should be given coverage commensurate with its importance to the whole. Some items warrant only mention in the calendar of events or in the news briefs or sports shorts columns. Many events or topics relate to so few persons that they must be left out to make room for bigger stories. If motorcycling appeals to a small section of the student population and sports car rallies or water skiing to a larger number, then a regular column on cycles and an occasional article on the other activities would be out of balance. The fact that members of the publication's staff are in the chess club should not call for repeated stories on the exploits of those few persons at the expense of recognizing, say, what some 75 Future Farmers are doing.

In addition to sequence, the amount of space allotted a section should reflect the general philosophy behind a publication. Whatever image the staff is attempting to project, the editors will do well to consider each phase of content in light of its relative importance or interest to the potential readership. Departments should be allotted space that reflects the proportionate interest in the subject matter. If music rates high with the student body, but the editors are into sports, the space given each should be weighed against the proportion of interest among the general audience. This does not mean that if a survey indicated that 60 percent of the students would like to see a gossip column, over half the space should be given to such trivia. Editors of any publication must hold to their own set of standards for high-quality content, and gossip does not merit any of the expensive space in a school publication. The editorial standards should include fair play and putting the reader's welfare first. Persons entrusted with instruments of communication should not use them for personal gain or to promote special projects of limited importance.

CONTENT ORIENTATION

Articles that "tell it better" by giving the readers information they need or want and can use immediately usually are based on current interests and activities. If the basic aim is to inform, to educate, and to entertain, the relationship is enhanced by articles about music, movies, plays, art or photo exhibits, car rallies, bike trails, or anything of special interest to the select audience of the publication. Information the readers can use becomes education if they make any use of it. Stories about hobbies, pleasure pursuits, where to go, what to do, how to do it, what it is . . . offer useful information.

Content ideas can come from any school source: rules, riots, record of events, rumors. National, world, or local events may have a definite effect on a particular locale. One might relate a situation to the school reader by showing its effects on the local scene. Some school publications have done this successfully with gasoline shortages, economic problems, ecological trends, and the metric system. Another device to localize a national or broad news subject is to survey students and teachers for reactions, suggestions, or projections.

Concentrating on the interests of the readers can suggest any number of articles and the slant that would make a subject an appropriate one for a publication. Crime that does not relate is not news material for the school publication, but shoplifting, cheating, drug use, rape, bike thefts, and truancy affect the student population. Articles about cruise ships probably would not hit home, but hitchhiking, European youth hostels, foreign-study tours, Amtrak, and vacation possibilities would appeal. Hobbies provide good subject matter in themselves, and when the article features a person who has achieved some distinction in pursuit of a hobby, the copy can become even more alive and interesting.

Members of publications staffs should read and observe daily to keep abreast of copy possibilities. The pages of any daily newspaper can offer more story ideas than a staff could compile for a single issue. Watching what goes on at school and in the area should provide strong indications of topics that interest the specific population. For example, at the time Gerald Ford was suddenly propelled into the Presidency of the United States, he made a trip to the family's residence in Virginia and emerged with two items, which he personally carried to the White House. What were they? His favorite golf jacket and his high-school yearbook. The first item might bring forth a sports feature about "friendly" old clothes for which people form attachments. The high-school yearbook notation should be a boon to student journalists. A survey of parents might reveal how many still have their books, how often they look at them, and whether they know exactly where the books are at the moment. The story would have even more impact if a return canvass were made in a week and the same parents were asked if the first query had prompted them to dig up the books, and if so, how much time was spent with them. The resulting information might possibly be a factor in boosting sales of the school yearbook or at least provide some interesting bits of copy for the volume.

CURRICULUM COVERAGE

Among the in-school areas that offer potential subject matter are modes of transportation, methods of studying, fashion fads for clothing and grooming, after-school activities, individual sports, hobbies, pastimes, and whatever the young people are talking about or doing. School grade and club activities are usually well publicized, but often curriculum coverage is overlooked. The acquisition of knowledge is what school is about, and there should be some documenting of what goes on in the classrooms or in competitions that measure classroom accomplishment. Reporting on participation of students in speech and math tournaments, science and home economics fairs, foreign-language and journalism or English writing contests, or music competitions is an excellent way to include curriculum coverage and student names; but fun things such as skits in English or language classes or demonstrations in speech class, or the construction of string designs in geometry make excellent subjects for photo features. A group of pictures of girls learning archery in physical education can add a visual surprise for the reader and give the staff photographers some excellent practice in dramatic composition. School is primarily academic, and whenever the learning activities are enjoyable, the school publication should depict this aspect.

Frequently teachers do not realize that routine classroom activity is newsworthy. A case in point is the history teacher who repeatedly signed the reporter's beat sheet saying there was "no news from this department at this time," when each Friday some students were recreating segments of their current study of Revolutionary War days. One group of girls had acquired some 200-year-old recipes and prepared baked goods as nearly like those of the Pilgrims as possible. Their class had a feast, and it was a most enjoyable lesson period. Another group of students staged a "witch trial" in hilarious fashion. Experiments in the science department often are entertaining as well as educational. If a staff has an interest in finding out what is going on and the ability to record these events in a readable manner, curriculum coverage can be that with which the readers identify most. Such stories are an excellent way to include the names of the "Joe Blow" average persons in a publication. And it is the Joe Blows and Jane Does who make up the bulk of the readership in most schools.

COMMUNITY COPY

Community awareness will serve the staff with reader interest and copy ideas. Relating the school to the community, and vice versa, should be a prime target for the school publication. Telling the school story to parents and other citizens is part of the obligation. Dealing with local problems, accomplishments, and activities broadens the scope and adds dimension—makes the publication more real. One strong link that will serve to promote acceptance of the publication by the student population is the publicizing of student participation in community affairs. Many students do volunteer work in hospitals, for charity organizations, or in political campaigns. A number of students work in the community and contribute to the economy. Stories about school-related employment programs make good copy; so do stories about enterprising young people who occupy places in the working world. Young people are involved in the betterment of society through church or scouting activities. The school publication can make a significant contribution to the community by recognizing the work of the "good" youthful citizens. It also can serve the school population by examining areas for recreation and leisure-time pursuits. Some good school copy has been written on ideas for fun times on frugal budgets; stories explored various no-charge facilities such as libraries, parks, museums, municipal or corporate buildings open to the public, and areas in the community for research and education beyond the classroom—plants to tour, business libraries for special studies, films, speakers, or other programs available that might offer extensions to the school curriculum. The use of local citizenry for guidance in student affairs need not be limited to Junior Achievement or Explorer Scout groups. A publication staff might compile a roster of local experts who could speak to classes or offer guidance for student activities in innumerable areas.

Local business people might be asked to discuss community reaction to national news events. Career guidance in any area can offer pertinent information. Most business or professional people are happy to pass along tips on preparation and requirements for their particular field.

Perhaps one of the most interesting and contributory areas of community awareness might be a compilation of local history and folklore from senior citizens of long residence in the area. Because students' years are less than two decades, old timers' tales hold fascination if presented in a comparative light. It is not especially interesting to know on what date a school district was started, or when a building was built, unless the information includes something currently involving the reader for contrast. The fact that five students were in the first graduation class of a high school might startle no one, but if community growth is exhibited by including the current number of graduates with companion figures on total area population for the two eras, or total number of families, or houses, the modern student might find interest heightened. Sometimes long-time residents have old photographs that might be printed to illustrate their stories. Or they may have a collection of local artifacts from less modern times that would make good photographic subject matter. The people themselves would probably be very good prospects for personality features. As with any other subjects not directly connected with the students or the school, people portrayal must be "brought home," in some way related to student interests. Since almost everyone went to high school once, a natural peg is obvious, but the more ways the writer can connect the activities, the accomplishments, the drives and ambitions of the subject with those of the readers, the more effective can be the story.

OPINION MATTER

Editorial sections include "official" staff-attitude editorials plus as wide a range of individual opinion as a particular publication desires. Often the editor writes a regular column of comment. There is generally an effort to include letters from readers. Some staffs have found it expedient to invite guest editorial writers to express their views. Interpretive articles often find their spot in the viewpoint section rather than with the "news." If much subjective interpretation or advocacy is included, the opinion section is the proper spot for it. Polls, surveys, and symposiums make excellent copy and provide avenues for including individual statements as well as relating news situations to the local scene. Establishing the services of an ombudsman, or intermediary, also can broaden the scope of problem-solving copy.

In a number of instances the interpretive article appears to be replacing the traditional editorial essay. Perhaps newsmagazine staffs become accustomed to writing longer articles and find the structure of the formal editorial too restrictive. More likely, there is a lack of talent available for this style of writing. Like news briefs, which must be tightly written to include the essential information in the smallest space, the editorial requires strong expression and crisp treatment to make its point in a few paragraphs. Frequently scholastic journalists spend too little time studying the art of editorial writing and fail to grasp the technique. A conference among the top echelon should precede the writing, if the piece is to represent the consensus of staff opinion. There should be no first person singular in an editorial—in a column with a by-line, yes—but never in an unsigned editorial. Since, ideally, this copy is to be presented in a wider column measure, the paragraphs can be a bit longer and the writing style a trifle more literary, but objectivity of approach and factuality of information must hold steadfast. Objectivity of approach means that the writer examines the situation from all angles before taking a stand. If all sides of the picture are not clearly understood, then calling for a specific action may well be courting disaster.

The publication that omits traditional editorials is missing an opportunity to exert leadership. Because the newsmagazine can reach the reader with its total content and establish a reputation for credibility through a policy of accuracy, completeness, and fair play, the publication stands the best chance of influencing the actions of the readers. Editorials should be an important part of the viewpoint content, not the last things written at press time. Editorials that relate to the big problems of the moment or the major news items have a built-in interest factor. The editorial offers the spot to call for specific action or attitude change on the part of the readers. If a well-written news analysis or interpretive article is in the same or a recent issue, the clout is intensified, but the longer article is not the spot best suited for advocating reader behavior.

Editorial subject lists should not include school spirit or cafeteria clean-up or smoking in the rest rooms, unless the staff has a strikingly new approach to these eternal head-knockers. In fact, there should not be a list of "suggested editorial subjects," because editorials should stem from current concerns. There should be a real "reason for being" for every editorial asking for the reader's attention, and the more pressing the issue, the more pertinent the subject as editorial material.

READER-CONCERN SUBJECTS

Explanatory features that appeal to teen-age readers include subjects that might arise from friction with parents or others in the adult world—runaways, alcoholism, traffic-ticket traps, marijuana laws, job restrictions, college requirements and costs, transportation, spending money, juvenile court, detention hall, school suspension, politics, or any number of contrasts between life-styles. Teens also are basically humane and are concerned about their less fortunate peers. They are attracted to stories about poverty, deprivation, and other injustices in their areas. In schools where no apparent "problems" exist and staffs feel there is little "news" to write about, much contribution to the community can be made by publicizing situations in areas where teens could contribute. If a school club or church group is going into the poverty areas to tutor children or offer supervised recreation on Saturdays, the staff has a ready-made story. If such activities are not happening, the enterprising staff can generate philanthropic programs by finding areas of need and promoting organization of such activity. If there is an existing teen hotline for callers in distress, publicity can give credit to a worthy cause and possibly recruit additional volunteers. Editors who are on top of things among the teen-agers in their area should seldom have to scratch for meaningful copy ideas. Such heavy reporting needs more time than straight news and light feature writing. Assignments for such long-range features should be made weeks or months before they are scheduled for publication. Good reporters need time to research the physical conditions, the philosophical or sociological aspects, and the people involvement in such all-encompassing accounts. There must be time for researching background information, gathering surface facts, interviewing persons involved, and for studied compilation of the articles. And there should be time for the completed story to be circulated among the editors, to garner reactions and test effectiveness. There should be time for the authors to rewrite their own copy; editors should limit their participation to suggestions and editing for style and errors. The original author benefits most from personally attending to the rewriting.

SOLICITED READER PARTICIPATION

Polls of students and teachers offer some of the easiest ways to gain copy that relates to current problems or events and involves a number of people. Conducting surveys can be a risky business, however, if much care is not taken with the wording of the instrument and the selection of the persons polled. Standard procedure for obtaining a "representative sampling" of a population from which to project a summation of the total opinion calls for a 10 percent cross section—10 percent of each segment of the whole. A representative sampling for a general school survey would be based on the breakdown numbers in each grade level for each sex. Ten percent of the seniors would not be representative if the number of boys and girls surveyed did not correspond respectively to their proportions of the total in the class. On the other hand, if the subject being examined had to do with participation in varsity sports, and only participants could correctly answer the questions, then the percentage of boys and girls to be surveyed would be designated by their corresponding number active in the athletic program.

Wording of questions should never lead pollees into preselected answers. It is easy to slant questions to produce desired answers, or to present the questions in such a way that pollees are subconsciously led into making untrue responses. Instruments for measuring public opinion should be constructed with absolute objectivity, as devoid as possible of any play on prejudices or emotional ties inherent in the pollees.

Writing stories from such polls calls for both analytical and imaginative techniques. The writer must be able to compile the statistics and read trends or significant patterns that develop in the figures, but must also be able to communicate the results in a lively, interesting style. Survey stories that contain too many references to percentages are difficult for the reader to follow. Using "picturable" comparisons, such as two out of three, over half, or one in ten, makes for easier absorption of the mathematical concepts.

Not all poll stories need be based on representative samplings to produce good copy. The only rule here is not to represent informal polls as "random samplings," a term that connotes scientific research, and not to project conclusions from the unscientific surveys. Asking a few questions of a group of students who chance to pass by a specific spot during the noon hour can produce some interesting material, but if the only students likely to pass that spot at that time are of one grade level, there is little "chance" or random element in the selection of pollees. The story could still offer interesting results on one age group's reaction to a given set of questions, but it would not be correct to project their responses to those older or younger than themselves. Polls or surveys of such informal nature might be accompanied by photographic coverage—sort of a reporter-on-the-street questioning of passersby for brief reactions to a current event. If conducted on a regular basis, and especially if given photographic emphasis, such stories may become popular features.

Symposium-type interviews can be conducted among persons with appropriate background to offer significant responses. Symposiums are based on longer reactions from authoritative persons. A case study on, say, school dropouts might include only two or three persons who reveal their reasons for leaving school and their current attitudes and reactions to their resulting situation. In stories of this nature, names might be withheld or changed. For less personal subject matter, names of authority figures should be printed to give credence to the content. Photographs here would add considerable interest.

An intermediary or ombudsman is one who intercedes with an authority for a person who has a problem or a question. In such a column in the newsmagazine, one person receives questions from readers and then interviews authoritative sources. The column writer serves as a liaison between persons with problems or discontent and the authority figures with answers or possible solutions. The ombudsman seeks out the authority rather than attempting to be authoritative. The credibility stems from the impartiality of approach.

With some or all of the aforementioned avenues to convey opinion and inject reader reaction, the newsmagazine has the opportunity to offer a real forum for exchange of ideas. The editors have the responsibility of leading off with strong editorials, of inviting contributions loudly and often, of working to make reader reaction important, and of striving to include as many varied opinions and attitudes as are representative of the publication's readers. The subject matter, the substance, and the dignity and forcefulness with which such material is presented will be key factors in the effectiveness of the section.

Sports Copy

Sports writing for school publications is too often riddled with partisan comment. Especially in the newsmagazine, because comment columns are more prevalent here, there should be definite lines of demarcation between sports news accounts and sports commentary. News stories about upcoming or past events should contain attribution to some authority for subjective statements. If the team did poorly, let one of the players or the coach tell why, not the reporter. If prospects look good, laud the team's efforts in comment columns, not factual accounts.

Sports pages warrant bold, explosive design. The copy should follow through with colorful, well-paced writing. As with any journalistic composition, the lead paragraph is most important in attracting the reader and securing his interest. Since this is a section in the school publication, all readers will assume the team mentioned is *their* team unless otherwise identified. It should not be necessary to begin all stories with the school or mascot name. It is, however, important that the sport be identified, and whether it is the boys', girls', varsity, or other classification of team status. Sports accounts, particularly of seasonal competitions running for some length, are more interest-packed when focused on the future or upcoming event than on previous games. Past game coverage should decrease in space allotment as the time distance increases. The more recent the game, the earlier it is treated in a composite sports cover story. The amount of space devoted to each game decreases as the time lapse grows, and coverage moves down in the story. A certain amount of sports jargon may lend a special air of locker-room excitement to such stories, but for the most part the language should be clear and straightforward. Colorful writing calls for use of action verbs, word-picture descriptions, identifiable comparisons, and crisp, direct sentences; fancy word-coinage and language manipulation is not necessary to achieve vibrant sports copy. On the other hand, too simple a style, with much repetition by use of short, choppy sentences, demands nothing of the imagination and bores the reader with its drudging pace.

When quotes are used in sports stories, just as in any other kind of story, those enclosed in quotation marks should be the exact words of the speaker. Write quotes as people talk, not as people write. One of the weaker beginnings for a sports story (just behind dates of old games and school or mascot titles) is a long quotation that does not sock the reader with new information or unusual phraseology. Paraphrasing and summarizing quotations is a more interesting way to handle routine statements. Save the quotation marks for significant expressions that reveal true information or reflect the personality or attitude of the person speaking. A closing direct quote is good; it has a tendency to give the reader a feeling of closeness with the subject in the story. But a weak quotation at the beginning creates an impression of weakness in the interviewee that detracts from the force of the information. Interspersing direct quotes is a valuable device for adding spice and reality to the written piece, but unless the quotations actually add information or characterize the mood, they fail to meet this function.

Good sports coverage, magazine style, includes the usual factual accounts of competitions, future and past, of team schedules and personnel. Such coverage gives a proportionate notation to minor sports and backup teams as well as the varsity squad. A column of comment written either by a single author or by a series of persons with expertise in various fields, or an edited selection of reader comments and questions, fosters reader identification with the section. Additional feature material for the sports section stamps the newsmagazine hallmark. Group and individual athletics and outdoor activities offer more ideas for good feature stories than a single publication might find space for in a year's issues. Naturally there are the obvious seasonal sidebars about training rules, physical-fitness drills, practice equipment, and film review sessions for the various teams. There are the in-depth reports on state competition rules and rule-makers, the college recruiting of senior stars, inspirational tales of graduates who have made it on the college field, and the coach's background and philosophy of guiding sportsmanship. Yet there are many areas for excellent copy outside the stars of the school varsity competition. Individuals who enjoy participation sports such as tennis, swimming, golf, hockey, horseback riding, backpacking, skating, hiking, surfing, bike riding, skiing, boating, snowmobiling, or hunting and fishing offer tremendous adventure story possibilities. There may be students or teachers who ride horses in shows or rodeos, who train falcons or hunting dogs, who work on ranches weekends learning to bulldog cattle or rope steers. Many students spend out-of-school hours at wrestling, judo, karate, ballet, tumbling, or gymnastics classes. Perhaps there are neighborhood soccer, hockey, or baseball leagues that draw a number of interested students, or church basketball leagues, or "Y" programs for groups or individuals. Sports car rallies and auto crosses make good sports copy, as do bike-riding events, staged or spontaneous. If any local professionals happen to have relatives in the school, inspiring personality stories might reveal some secrets of success to the interest and benefit of the readers.

Sports feature material can be timely without being immediately current. A tale of last summer's adventure on the wilderness trail in the mountains will appeal most any time, but it may have more impact in the spring when young people are making summer plans. Camping stories are good any time that camping out is a physical possibility.

Headlines

One of the happiest areas of difference between the newsmagazine format and that of newspapers is in the wording and arrangement of headlines. As mentioned previously, the headline need not follow the standard rules of containing a verb, summarizing the lead paragraph, neatly filling the space above the story, and so forth. The magazine head becomes a title, imparting the subject of the story, piquing the reader's interest, and subtly conveying the tone of the article. That last characteristic is a key one: the tone or attitude of the writing. Unless the article is particularly austere or controversial, a bit of humor in the wording or whimsy in the arrangement can increase reader enjoyment.

During the 1973–74 school year, interest on campuses across the country was running high over "streaking," dashing unclothed through public places. Articles on the fad brought forth a rash of enjoyable expressions extending the mood of jest on which the whole scene was based. "STREAKING—the naked truth," "the bare facts," or "nothing to hide," are plays on words, familiar phrases used in a new light. The *Cadet Call* of Marmion Military Academy in Aurora, Illinois, offers cadets a challenge to express their humor through literary devices: "Academic cribbers connive to thrive" for an article on cheating; "Satanic resurrection: Black Sabbath still raising hell" for a review of a recording by the sinisterly named rock group; and "Where has all the money gone? Outlook bleak for college aid" on an examination of grants available at area colleges. The same group had visual fun with a headline on the story of a study in the economics class. The head was displayed on graph paper with sections placed at right angles to indicate a rising and falling market. The kicker, "Let's make a deal," rode over: "Econ classes lose money in stock market." *The Anvil* of the Spring Branch Memorial High School in Houston, Texas, arranged a railroad track behind a story on Amtrak. For an analytical look at senior boys' attempts to paint a neighboring school, which ended in a fight between partisan groups from each school, they wrote: "Bury my heart at Northbrook and look at my wounded knee." A three-personality story about brothers on the track team was headed "See how they run." A story on the girls' track team ran under "Ms. Sprint dons cleats." How about: "Quadraphonia not stereo-type," or "Quarter system squared away," or "Metric system: inching up on American life," or the head for a story about one of their students in the American Field Service program: "An American broad in Slavonski Brod"?

The staff of the *Hobachi* of Redlands (California) High School obviously enjoys headline writing and design. Theirs was the "naked truth" head for a streaking story. For one of a series of articles on teen alcoholism, they used "Stalking the fermented grape."

The All-Important Content

"Cultivating contented cannabis" ran over a botanical explanation of the marijuana plant; and "Behind closed cums" introduced an editorial on access to cumulative folders. "The Redlands connection, an inside look at the drug situation in Redlands and at RHS" headlined an in-depth report. These student journalists particularly enjoy graphics design and present a publication so visually magnetic that their enjoyment projects from the pages. A sports column, "The other side of sports," ran under a stacked heading doubled over with one side reflecting the other in reverse. Another called "Out of bounds" was boxed, with the last few letters spilling out of "bounds." Their news-notes page was dotted with tiny black ants in the issue carrying the story of the drama department's production of "Alluwishous, the Eight-legged Ant." The drawing of a broken light bulb over "Watt's up?" was dropped into a story about the energy crisis. The type in "Traditions on the way out" faded from 100 percent intensity to a weak 30 percent from the first "T" to the last. "Asphalt, asphalt everywhere . . . and not a place to park" was set off, with its story, by rows of cars drawn as a traffic jam around the corner of the column.

It is much easier to tell others how to write than it is actually to compose good material. When the writer is inhibited by too many do's and don'ts, spontaneity is restricted. To be readable, writing should be free—not stilted or restrained. If it is too stiff and scholarly it probably will repel readers as rapidly as if the grammar and spelling are incorrect. Each person must develop an individual writing style—a manner of expression that comes naturally, without strain. Facility with language is a definite prerequisite. A sound vocabulary is needed, but not necessarily an enormous one. Readers prefer material they can understand over that which sends them to the dictionary. Use words everyone will understand, and in the proper context. Magazine article writing, unless purposely fictional, deals with facts and reality. Information should be correct, facts reported accurately, and the viewpoint undistorted. The object is to "tell it better." "Better" means more fully, more clearly, more informatively. To make the writing more interesting, magazine staffers sharpen their writing styles and use of words, but they do not add or distort facts. The by-line should appear as a mark of achievement signifying that the writer has accomplished the task with exceptional flair, rather than as an excuse for opinionated comments in so-called factual accounts.

Summarizing, the all-important content in newsmagazines:

1. Is grouped by subject areas for reader convenience.
2. Contains factual, accurate documentation of events for the present and future audiences.
3. Reflects proportionately the general and specific interests of the readership.
4. Deals with topics of genuine interest to a significant number of readers.
5. Offers information of value to the readers.
6. Offers leadership through interpretive and editorial material.
7. Encourages reader participation.
8. Separates reporter opinion from factual matter.
9. Cites authorities for statements of fact or opinion in news articles.
10. Is written with the aim of being interesting and amusing as well as informative and educational.
11. Is carefully prepared for accuracy, impartiality, completeness, correctness of grammar, and brightness of writing style.

Chapter VI

QUALITY CONTROL

Quality control is a vital phase in the operation of most successful manufacturing enterprises. Someone must check each piece of factory output to be sure it meets the standards and specifications of company policy so that all products are consistently excellent.

A thorough check for quality in each edition of a publication is necessary to maintain standards set out in the policy and format. Both visual and verbal aspects of the content should be tested against a rigid set of controls that are basic to the publication.

Quality control for the content of a publication should come long before the copy reaches the paste-up stage. Editing is a vital function of any good publication. Each reporter should thoroughly check the copy before submitting it to the editor. Editors are responsible for seeing that every piece of writing is accurate, well written, and conforms to the stylebook. The stylebook for rules of expression, spelling, abbreviation, and the like should be followed as carefully as the format and typographical specifications. The stylebook for a particular publication should be detailed to the minuteness of punctuation and abbreviations of campus organizations and spelling of local names.

FUNCTIONS OF EDITING

Good copy editing can improve poor writing by adding clarity and rhythm and by correcting grammar. Copy editing adds the perfectionist touch. The copyreader checks first for accuracy of facts. Errors in print are for all to have and to hold from this day forward. Some publications give reporters assignment sheets with notations on what a story should contain and require these sheets with the story notes to be turned in with the finished copy. If there is a place on the sheet for the source of information to sign, then the editors should feel confident the facts therein are substantiated. Yet small details can slip by both reporters and copy editors. If the story states that a car wash is to be held on Saturday, March 9, and the calendar shows Saturday to be March 8, the potential customers will not know whether the car wash is to be on Saturday or Sunday. Any numerical or statistical material should be double-checked for accuracy. The editor is expected to know everything or to know what to question in the stories crossing the copydesk, and to seek some authority for verification. Once an item is in print, it is permanent and public—you get all the mistakes back, and every error is one more chip off your credibility. Advertisements, too, must be checked in every detail, especially for correct firm name, address, phone number, and product pricing. Advertisers often refuse to pay for space ordered if incorrect information reduces or negates the effectiveness of the ad.

Check Points for Copy Editors

The copyreader, in improving the clarity of the writing, checks grammar and eliminates unnecessary repetition. Agreement in number, gender, and tense is vital to smooth writing and is often the most flagrantly violated rule of grammar. Common usage in oral language does not always make correct written expression. One should not use a singular subject and plural object, as "Everyone use their best grammar." Present-tense writing should not suddenly lapse into past tense, or future, without a transition phrase to explain the change. If a compound sentence is begun in the infinitive, it should be completed in the same form. Parallelism is also important for nouns, adjectives, and adverbs. Sentence structure in related material is more effective if there is parallelism. Some unschooled writers employ clichés or cute devices on which to "hang" their material. One, in writing on "success," employed each letter to key a phrase for each point to be made. Had this author used parallel construction for these key-point sentences, each beginning with the next letter in his thesis, the trite device might have stood up. However, since there was no similarity in structure among the key-point sentences, persons attempting to use the book in a study group had difficulty remembering each succeeding point. Such "M-O-T-H-E-R" writing is so camp that it must follow the perfect pattern established by the song if it is to be accepted. If writing is to impart information the reader will make use of, then it should be as clear and digestible as possible. The writer has the obligation to hold to good grammatical usage to aid the reader in absorbing and retaining the information.

The copy editor also hones the writing for conciseness. A good editor can sharpen a piece of writing by trimming excess verbiage, eliminating side-track addenda, and keeping the focus on the single thrust of the article. Such paring usually makes the individual piece more interesting and the whole publication more exciting.

Quality writing depends not only on correct and imaginative use of language, but on thoroughness of research. Care for accuracy and completeness is as vital to quality writing as adeptness with the language. The thorough reporter researches every possible angle for facts contributing to the completeness of an article, carefully noting the source from which each fact is gleaned. The competent writer exercises equal care in organizing the material and documenting the sources in the article, and presents the material in understandable, interesting prose.

Writers who have not absorbed the fundamentals of grammar and language usage cannot communicate as well or as grippingly as those who are adept with word arrangement. Many young writers confer impossible powers upon inanimate objects, such as "Friday saw failure for the Forest five in their efforts at the State basketball championship." Friday cannot see. Friday can dawn; it can blow in or fade away, but Friday can neither see, nor speak, nor control its weather. Student writers often back into sentences with phrases that do not relate to the subject of the sentence, causing the reader to ponder the source of the action. "Walking down the road, the boy saw the man and his dog" had better mean the boy was walking, though the reader may not be sure. It is difficult to concentrate on the action when one must wrestle with the author's meaning. Clarity, conciseness, and continuity are essential components of quality writing.

Tools for Copy Reading

Copy editors will find *The Elements of Style,* by William Strunk, Jr., and E. B. White, an invaluable ally in sharpening meaning and brevity of writing. The publication's stylebook, a current dictionary, and "Strunk and White" provide solutions for most problems in composition. Every reporter should be required to read the small volume on a regular basis. Mr. Strunk's attitude is set forth on page ix in the introduction:

> Vigorous writing is concise. A sentence should contain no unnecessary words, a paragraph no unnecessary sentences, for the same reason that a drawing should have no unnecessary lines. . . . This requires . . . that every word tell.

One important element in speeding the reader's comprehension is avoiding confusion from inconsistencies. Stylebooks were invented to help the writers for a publication know how to communicate dates, time of day, months, money figures, ages, distances, scores, quantities, contractions, abbreviations, titles, and locations. Because most newspapers subscribe to wire services for the bulk of their copy, the majority of them have standardized on the style adopted by both the Associated Press and United Press International. Many magazines use the same universal stylebook. Others have set forth their own rules of expression. Some use the basic tenets in the AP–UPI stylebook with additions or modifications. But every publication of any size has prescribed practices for handling words that can be communicated more than one way. It is important that each writer know the intricacies of the publication's style rules; it is paramount that the copyreaders pore over each piece of copy to be sure that it conforms to all rules. The reader will appreciate not being startled by sudden shifts in the use of recurring words or symbols. If details of a coming program are written 8:00 P.M. and $4.00 one time and 8 p.m. and $4 (or four dollars) another time, the reader will be subconsciously disturbed by the discrepancy. Such distractions hamper comprehension and diminish the reader's sense of identification with the publication.

The same holds for misspelled words, faulty punctuation, and bad grammar. Preciseness of language, consistency of expression, and accuracy of facts should be part of every writer's every effort. When these are lacking in an article, the copyreader must supply them if quality is to be maintained.

Copyreaders have a set of commonly used symbols for making corrections speedily. Most printers accept the standard copyreaders' marks found in general journalism textbooks; some, however, have specific methods they prefer. Each staff should inquire of its print shop what symbols and marks are to be used. Copyreaders' marks include symbols for making corrections, deletions, and additions and for indicating typographical specifications—kinds of letters, paragraph indentations, spacing, and the like. A large chart showing the symbols and their usage should be displayed in the copy working area where all can be guided by it. In any case, all persons who use copyreading marks should have a chart for handy reference.

Marking type specifications on a piece of copy includes making sure that the paragraphs are short enough to hold the reader's interest, are varied in length to offer visual appeal, and are properly arranged in the story to maintain continuity. Especially important is that the lead be short, even if the completed thought requires as many as three paragraphs. Overlong leads discourage the reader from even beginning to read.

If the type specs for a publication have been delineated, and every writer submits copy typed to a countable line length, the estimating of column inches for each piece should be relatively simple. Copy editors must know in more detail how to estimate copy length. They must be able to take copy typed at one measure and figure the space it will require at any other spacing. They must be able to visualize completed typography in a given space and know how to mark type specifications for the printer. The copy editor should be in charge of the "budget" sheet, that chart on which all stories are listed with number of inches and column measure. This inventory of copy being set at the printer's and the list of pictures and their finished sizes is what the page planners have to work with to assign places for stories while the typesetter is at work. Making use of this interim time for allotting content and plotting display can help avoid last-minute panic over clashes of facing pages or incompatibility of copy and adjacent advertising.

Role of Proofreading

When the copy is back from the typesetter, proofreading becomes the focus of quality control. Professional proofreaders work in pairs, checking every mechanical detail of the set copy. The ancient printer's rule, "Proof must conform to copy," still holds. Typesetters are obliged to reproduce copy exactly as it comes to them. If a word is misspelled by the writer and missed by the copyreader, it should come out on the proof misspelled the same way. Printers usually charge for "customer corrections"—changes from the original copy after proof has been submitted. Very many such extra charges, and the staff should realize that quality control must begin with the writer and the copyreader. Whether proofreaders work in pairs, reading aloud, or solo checking back to original copy when any unusual error or deviation appears, it is important that more than one person check each proof. There is a tendency by persons who have read a piece of copy before to read lightly on proof and to miss mistakes. If the author is among the proofreaders, that person might be first to read the galley, especially if the copy was retyped before sending it to the print shop. Just remember, changes in copy should have been made *before* the printer began to set the type. When corrections must be made after copy is already set in type, the proofreader must endeavor to involve as few lines as possible. When misspelled words or names appear, usually the correct number of spaces are involved and only one word or a single line need be replaced. For corrections involving changes that are longer or shorter than the portion in error, try to add or subtract words or characters to come out even with the next line or two. Avoid any change in meaning, but attempt to require as little resetting of the copy as possible. These new lines will have to be integrated by the page layout crew, and each separate piece of body text should be perfectly aligned at the edges with the rest of the column and the lines of type even with all the others on the page.

Details in Pasting-up

When long galleys of a story are to be cut up for arrangement on the page, some form of key is helpful to keep the paragraphs in proper succession. Numbering on the back lightly or affixing a numbered tab to each separate portion can help to prevent jumbling paragraphs. Many good articles have been weakened in school publications because the makeup person paid more attention to design than continuity of content in pasting-up.

If some bit of type or graphics device is to have special treatment in the photolithography or plate burning stage, and is affixed to the paste-up on an overlay or flap, instructions should be clearly indicated on the flap, and space markings should show position on the dummy with small right angles in litho blue pencil defining exact placement of the material. Printers do not purposely change your instructions, but extraneous material may be removed from the page dummy for the special processing, and print-shop workers may not know exactly what you had in mind for it.

Format consistency comprises those small details that identify a publication and maintain its stability through a variety of page designs. The publication's philosophy and policy will be reflected in the visual aspects of the format as well as in the verbal expressions of the copy. The small details of skeletal planning—margins, folios, column structures, standing heads, logo, cover plan, headline schedule, and ads—serve as the solid foundation on which the special adventures in design are based.

Art directors, production managers, and editors should be alert for the minor details that form this foundation of consistent excellence. Publication staffs who have detailed "grids" for planning and executing page layouts stand a better chance of achieving the desired consistency. These gridded dummy sheets should define the margin areas, page number and folio placements, column structure(s), and even ad placement and photo bleed trim area in some instances. With places clearly marked for these items, the paste-up crew is less likely to omit the vital details of department identifiers or folios. Some publications have dummy sheets marked for lines of type numbering to the maximum line count for each column. If not so specific as that, at least the grids should have horizontal lines no fewer than four to an inch in order to keep the lines of type perfectly horizontal. The mark of the finer publications will be alignment of all lines of type on every lateral across the entire spread. For instance, if three columns of type on the left-hand page all reach the bottom margin, and two columns on the facing page also fill, all five lines should be straight across as if an imaginary line ran under them. And anywhere on the pages, all lines in that plane should rest squarely on an imaginary line straight across the spread. When lines of type in adjacent columns are not perfectly even, the white space between lines creates a wavy distraction.

FINE POINTS WITH GRAPHICS

Straightness of line is important for the entire publication, not only in headlines and paragraphs of the body copy, but even in the smaller fragments such as folios and photo credits. All lines of type, save for special-effect arrangements, should be parallel with the top and bottom edges of the page. All vertical lines and white spaces between columns should be plumb with the vertical edges. Gutters or "rivers" of white space that separate columns and other elements on the pages should be not only straight, but even. As with the margins, no type should violate these white areas; they should be perfect rules of white, unwavering and unbending as the black-ruled lines must be. When rules, whether tapes or artist-drawn, are to appear on the pages, they should be absolutely straight. Mitered corners give a more finished appearance than butted corners. Mitered corners are achieved by overlapping the intersecting strips and then cutting both tapes with a razor knife at a 45-degree angle slanted toward the inside of the box. The strips of tape meet at 45-degree angles in the corners rather than having one square-edged piece run beyond the next in "T" fashion. If strips of tape are overlapped in a T at the corners, this thickness may cause a shadow when the page is photographed for reproduction. The gridded dummy sheet offers the advantage of printed lines to help guide the artists in keeping the rules plumb and unwavering.

The grid defines the margins and the page edge. Nothing should ever be in the margin area unless it is a bleed piece of art. When a bleed is indicated by the layout artist, the control checker should ascertain if there is an extra quarter-inch for trimming on the photograph or drawing. Bleeds are printed beyond the trim edge of the sheet in order to avoid any slip of white showing, so the artwork must have some trimmable area on the bleeding edges to avoid cutting into the vital content. It is important for the makeup staff to know how the paper is fed into the press. Sometimes the printer cannot accomplish a bleed photo on the gripper edge of the page. The staff should know which pages are printed together, not only for paste-ups, but in case color is to be used; because often the same color can be added to other pages printed simultaneously for little or no increase in cost. Cover color can usually carry over to the back page, whether as a wrap-around design or in a separate treatment.

All art being sent for reproduction should be crisp, clean, and uncluttered. If framing is to be part of the pictorial display, the boxes are drawn or taped on the paste-up; for pictures to stand alone, windows are pasted down in the exact position and shape desired. Any crooked or wavy lines or sloppy corners will be transferred to the printing plate. When construction paper or other red or black material is used to create clear windows for stripping-in screened photos, any fuzzy edges or crooked sides will be reproduced in the finished product. Smudges or scratches on the windows or the finished art will also show up on the halftone negatives. Marks on the back of photographs often break the emulsion on the face side and show up as flaws in the pictures. Among the duties of the control checker is that of checking the crop marks on the photos and noting the reduction or enlargement in relation to the space marked on the dummy. Only one set of crop marks should be on the prints sent to the shop. If page designers have changed their minds or made corrections on the prints, care should be taken to instruct the photolithographer as to which indications to follow. The photolithographer may not have access to the dummy sheets to figure out what is correct. There should be no guesswork on the printer's part; instructions should be perfectly clear. Photos themselves should be sharp, contrasty, and free of dust or dirt marks.

HARMONY IN DISPLAY

Headlines should be associated with the stories. The lines of the head should be anchored together, and there must be some visual relationship between the head and its story. Typography for the head should be in harmony with the mood of the piece, and the design should assist the mood artistically when feasible. Pages should always be checked against those that complete the spread. Frequently a well-designed page loses its effectiveness because of conflict with the other side of a spread. Always check facing pages to be sure they complement each other.

Ad content and copy must also not conflict. When ads are dummied in, notation should be made of the products emphasized. Departmental content should be considered in ad placement to make sure ads are appropriate. An article about saving money by making your own clothes is certainly not a good companion for dress-shop ads. Such editorial conflicts probably represent the best argument for those who advocate all-ad pages, which are offensive to most advertisers. Ideally, the makeup staff should avoid placement of conflicting ads, such as two banks or two restaurants, on the same page or spread. One acceptable avenue around both this dilemma and the advertisers' objections to all-ad pages is to play up the conflict, so to speak, by grouping like ads into "directories" with significant headings and continuity of display. A restaurant guide becomes a reader service, as do an entertainment guide, an investment or financial directory, or a list of self-improvement courses such as lessons in judo, karate, driving, guitar, etc. Such a page can become a reader-interest page, with exceptional visual appeal, rather than a page that carries the financial burden of the publication but is skipped over, unread, by the consumer because conflicting display was repelling.

Quality-control watchdogs should be on the job all the way through the final preparation of the boards—the finished layouts of the pages ready for the camera. In some smaller page size publications, printers prefer boards of two pages side by side, which will become a single negative for printing. Only in the case of the center spread and the back page and cover are these two pages that print together the pages that will face each other in the finished product. Presses that print two pages at a time handle the sheets vertically; these, when folded, become half-size pages on which the vertical runs in the opposite direction. For a 16-page publication, the back page would be pasted up to the left of the cover. Page 2 would be on the left side of the board with page 15 on the right half. Page 14 would be printed to the left of page 3, and so on, with even-numbered pages always on the left and odd-numbered on the right. A number of production variables (kind and size of press, number and size of pages, etc.) influence the imposition of pages for printing. Each staff should consult its printer for instructions as to page layout and groupings. Then some quality-control person should check for this arrangement and compare pages that will face each other in the finished publication for compatibility.

Finishing Touches

Because the final paste-ups are to be photographed as they are received at the print shop, neatness is vital. All ink smudges, glue smears, type slips, and border sloughs will show up on the negative. Unless the printer has a kindhearted retoucher who will paint out your mistakes, they will appear, graphically and indelibly, on your finished printed piece.

Most printers, although contracting with clients for camera-ready copy (meaning pages pasted up ready for photographing, with windows or boxes correctly sized and placed for all screened photos or art work), will submit page proofs from the negatives before plates are burned. One definite advantage in quality control that letterpress publications have over their offset cousins is the facility with which changes can be made at the proof stage. With offset, additions must be stripped into the negative by mortising the page negative and placing the new material on film in the hole. Incorrect words and letters are too costly to correct at this stage. Isolated fragments of type that have slipped or fallen off can be fixed on the negatives if they are not too close to other elements. Cutting and stripping the lithographic film requires precision; it takes time and costs money. The best way to avoid this is to make sure that all elements are securely mounted on the paste-up. Reburnish waxed proofs, and make sure tips of small pieces such as credit lines are firmly anchored. All pages should be covered and placed in a container for the trip to the print shop.

The best practice for achieving quality control is to do it right the first time; check it over before sending it to the shop; keep it accurate; keep it clean.

To summarize, if the level of perfection in a publication is to be maintained:

1. Each reporter's copy will be accurate, well written, and in conformity with the stylebook.
2. Copy editors will check carefully for accuracy and correct style in details such as dates, figures, punctuation, and spelling as well as factuality of material and clarity of expression.
3. Production instructions will follow guidelines preferred by the specific print shop, and will be clean and clear to avoid misunderstandings and make-overs.
4. Galley proofs will be checked as diligently as original copy, by several persons.
5. Care will be taken to keep all lines and edges straight and sharp.
6. Someone will check every page for format details—folios, departmental identifiers, typographical specialties.
7. Paste-ups will be checked before being sent to the shop to assure visual compatibility of facing pages and editorial compatibility between advertising and text material.
9. All elements on final paste-ups will be securely attached (burnished, if waxed) and the pages carefully covered and placed in a container for transporting to the print shop.

Chapter VII

SPECIAL TECHNIQUES AND EQUIPMENT

Some tips on accomplishing good graphics design have been scattered throughout this book where their inclusion seemed appropriate. The business of preparing publications for reproduction is a constantly improving exercise. New equipment and materials are introduced continually that do a better job than some currently in use. But most customers of the printing trade must make do with less sophisticated tools. This chapter will discuss some techniques or tricks that might help to accomplish a more precise and/or exciting graphics display and some simple equipment with which a staff might find this goal attainable.

Alignment

The most valuable human asset the makeup staff can have is a keen eye—the ability to see what looks best in aligning and spacing printed materials. In using hand-set rub-on type, for instance, the round letters such as capital O, C, and G actually look aligned with the others in a word when these characters extend slightly beyond the baseline. Spacing between letters cannot be mathematically predetermined as equal; the contour of each letter needs to be considered in line with those beside it and the spacing gauged optically. Two letters curving away from each other may need to be closer together than two with vertical ascenders or descenders adjacent to each other, as qp or db.

As mentioned in Chapter II, a page has a more professional appearance if the lines in each column across the spread are aligned so that the baseline or the white leading will follow a ruler straight across the entire area. Working on a preprinted grid helps accomplish this. When gridded paper is not available for pasting up a page or design, a plastic grid can be taped to the surface of the light table and provide guidelines on the quarter inch. These grids are a help even with prelined paste-up sheets, because they also have vertical guides every quarter inch to help in positioning photos or type that do not fall with the column structure printed on the paste-up sheet. Makeup artists should always work with square surfaces (light table, art board, or drawing table) and accurate T-squares and triangles to assist in making parallel lines parallel and perpendicular lines perpendicular.

Litho blue pencil marks on the paste-up sheet help to indicate where the various pieces are to be positioned before they are attached to the page. Whenever an overlay is attached to the paste-up, the page should be marked lightly in blue pencil at opposite corners of the exact spot the overlaid piece is to occupy. Overlays are necessary for precision in some special effects. Since they will be removed from the finished paste-up to be treated in another step, if you have not marked the exact position the overlaid material is to occupy, the printer will have to put it where he thinks he remembered it. An overlay is a separate sheet, preferably of see-through material, which is attached to the finished board in such a way that the heading, or trim, or whatever portion is to receive special treatment is positioned on the cover sheet in the precise spot where it is to appear on the finished page. If the staff wants a portion of the page display to have special treatment, such as screening or tinting, and does not make an overlay, then the printer will have to mask the rest of the page to shoot this portion separately, and time charges may be incurred. There may also be some time loss, because the single piece must be handled twice instead of two separate parts being processed simultaneously. Register marks (crosses or other symbols) are used to indicate precise placement of separate pieces. These marks are placed on both pieces in the trim area beyond the margin. Quality printing houses can achieve perfect register of elements from separate negatives or printing plates. When register is off, precision is lost, as when the Sunday color funnies appear with Little Orphan Annie's yellow hair outside the lines of her curly locks. If perfect register is not part of your print shop's standard practices, avoid graphics that demand such careful handling.

Accents

In order to call attention to special articles or pictorial matter, typographical devices can be added. Techniques for unusual treatment may be executed by the staff or in the photomechanical process. That is not to say that white space may not still be the most effective method of setting a story apart from the rest, but on occasion more graphic treatment is in order for special emphasis.

Accents on Reading Matter

When more than one story appears on a page, the makeup person must help the reader decide which to read first, which is the more important. Sometimes a screened background will do this, or a box or border may be used to set the story off, or white space may be used to frame it and attract attention. Perhaps even an especially dramatic headline will accomplish the feat. Only the eye can ascertain what arrangement in the space is best for the overall design—maintaining balance and readability in a pleasing composition. The main item need not necessarily go at the top left; a type device can make it stand out. To indicate a screened background for a type block, an overlay showing the exact position will assure precision. If the staff does not furnish an overlay, simply calling for a screened background by percentage (20 to 40 percent is best) with blue-penciled instructions on the paste-up (preferably in the adjacent margin area) can accomplish this. The printer will make a mask and register it with the type block, but he may charge for his time. If the screen is to be bordered or specially shaped, it is important for the staff to furnish an overlay for precision. Overlays can be made with special film-on-plastic sheets, but these cost considerably. Sturdy tracing paper can be used, or even plain white writing paper, so long as the register of overlay and paste-up is precise. Use a light box and T-square.

Accents on Photos

Special screens can be used over photographs to create striking effects. Most printers have screens on film to simulate mezzotints or steel etchings, and to create concentric circles, vertical or horizontal lines, and a number of other art effects. Use of these special effects (even the simple Ben Day screen) means an extra step in the plate-making process, called an overburn. The halftone image is first burned into the plate, then the special screen is positioned over the photo area and a second burn is made. This amounts to a surprint. Such techniques are routinely simple for photolithographers, and the charge for them is usually nominal. Screened sheets of acetate such as the rub-on letters are available and can be applied directly to the glossy print, thereby incorporating the pattern into the photo for a single plate burn. The printer's process will give a better-quality reproduction because the halftone image was transferred first, alone, and because there is the danger of leaving air bubbles between the acetate and the print, which will cause muddy spots to appear in the picture.

Some special effects in photographs can be accomplished in the darkroom. The most common is the high-contrast print, which eliminates tonal gradations and produces stark blacks and whites. The same effect can be achieved at no cost from the photolithographer by calling for an art conversion or line shot, wherein the photographer eliminates the screen and no dot pattern appears on the negative. This process drops out all gray tones and only blacks and whites are burned into the plate. Such pictures lend themselves well to layouts with reverse borders or boxes if the picture has a solid black side to meld with the black background.

School photographers can also produce positive "negatives," which print out in reverse and create a mysterious atmosphere for special occasions. Photographers can use a variety of materials, either over the enlarger lens or over the photographic paper, to produce unusual images: cheesecloth, wire meshes, nylon hose, transparent non-woven fabrics, even two negatives at once. Double-exposure prints are cheaper than two burns on the plate, and you can be more sure of positioning exactly where you want the images.

Remember, special effects are to be used for accent purposes. Be sure they are used on the items you want emphasized. Overuse will negate the impact. In this case, better too little than too much.

To add that extra dimension to photographs, a thin black border can be used to enclose the image. When this border finishes the photo precisely, an overburn on the plate is required. If border tape is attached to the glossy, it will be screened along with the image. For a crisp black line, place the tape on the paste-up instead of windows, to become part of the line negative. Then prepare an overlay, perfectly registered, showing the position of the halftones on a window, if your printer desires. Some printers make a positive film from the line negative and burn the halftones first and then the line work. This puts the trim line directly on the edges of the halftone image. When the border tape is prepared on an overlay, the problem of registering is considerably more difficult.

Another way to accomplish the crisp black border edge to halftones is to call for a velox and draw or tape the border directly on the print after pasting it on the final layout. A velox is a contact print from the screened negative used to burn the halftone image onto the plate. Some printers maintain that they can get equal quality on the printing plate by using the velox, which has converted the halftone image into a dot pattern, and skipping the step of stripping the screened negatives into the blank windows on the line negatives. Other printers claim that more detail is lost in "reshooting" the illustration in its screened image as a line shot. Only experimentation and consultation on the comparative costs can provide the solution for each individual staff within the physical capabilities of its facilities.

If a strip of white is to appear between the box and the actual screened image, the window must be made smaller than the outside box. This amounts to boxing the window on the paste-up. Imperfect register is not quite so apparent when this technique is applied, but the effect is not quite so startling, either.

If several photos are to be cut in odd shapes and used in a layout as a single visual element, the safest way to proceed is for the school darkroom to produce all glossies the same size and for the staff designer to cut and arrange the pieces on mounting paper so that the photolithographer can treat the whole as a single unit, a piece of "art." If some pieces must be reduced or enlarged at different percentages, there is always the chance that they will not come out to fit the spaces planned in the layout, or that the printer may not quite understand what the staff had in mind. Better that the school photographer do the reducing and enlarging to fit the diagram. The prints can be trimmed and pasted in the desired pattern and acetate tape used to separate the various parts. If a dark or gray dividing line is desired, the supply room should have something on hand. If white separation is preferred and white tape is not available, a double rule with opaque center may be substituted. Or the staff can make an overlay of the separation in black tape and this can be reversed at the printer's to produce a white line between pictures.

Windows on the paste-up dummy should be cut with a sharp razor knife against a heavy metal ruler with nonskid backing, especially if construction paper is used. This is the most inexpensive material available, but it is soft and the edges fuzz easily. Scissor cuts usually produce a ragged edge in this stock. And those ragged edges, as well as any irregularities in contour, will show up markedly in the final photograph. If the staff has access to a harder paper in red or black, a cleaner image may be achieved. A top-quality paper cutter in excellent condition will do a good job on larger pieces of window material. To be sure photographic images are placed in proper spots, it is wise to tag the glossy prints with the page number and the first few words of the cutline. Do not write on the window blocks, because the writing might appear in the window space and thereby be burned into the halftone image.

When artwork is being used, unless it is crisp black and white, call for a halftone; in screening, all details are picked up and some fine shadings might be lost in shooting a pencil drawing as a line shot.

Accents with Type

One of the best ways to integrate type and illustrations is to "wrap" the lines of text around the contour of the picture. This often means setting each line at a different pica measure to begin or terminate at a point near the outlined photograph or drawing. Since each line is approximately the same distance from the outline, the lines will vary in length as the outline changes. For very sophisticated computerized typesetters and for hot-type machinery, the staff can call for "line for line" typesetting by simply measuring the lines in picas and counting characters to fit the line length. If the drawing is to the right of the text, there will be little problem in fitting the pieces together. If, on the other hand, the illustration is on the left and copy is to be set flush right with a contoured margin at the left, there may be a bit more manipulation involved. Most printers, however, should be able to supply these lines. Unjustified copy yields equal word spacing and is quite readable, especially when all the lines begin on the same axis as in flush-left setting. If, however, your machinery is less sophisticated, more time will be needed by the operator in reprogramming for each line. One computer tape typist set 50 lines of such copy to encompass a circular photograph for a school; half were flush left and half flush right. The staff had counted every line by characters and so marked them by length in picas. The operator set each line, broke the punch tape and wrote the line length on it, set the next line, etc. Each of the fifty tapes had to be fed into the typesetting machinery separately, with the line length changed on each of the 50. Another school spent more hours cutting regularly set copy almost word by word to change the line lengths to follow a photo contour. Alignment of such type is a meticulous and tedious job. Students endeavoring to create contours with text type would do well to confer with their own print-shop operators to determine the most economical and efficient method of accomplishing their task. Schools with typesetting equipment operated by students may have some instruction booklets to assist in determining the procedure for their special machines, or the staff may need to contact the factory representative for some pointers. Many student staffs have found they can save money with their own typesetting equipment, once the initial costs of the machines are met. Depending on the sophistication of the machinery and the expertise of the student operators, the job can be as well done as in some professional establishments. The staff of the *Rincon Echo* in Tucson, Arizona, does the typesetting for its newsmagazine and has mastered the technique of contoured edges.

Setting headlines by hand to mesh with photographs calls for some "eyeballing" before any letters are actually rubbed in place. For headlines of unusual shape, do some character counting and some trial-and-error comps (pencil sketches as closely resembling the actual size and shape of the letters as possible to gauge the spacing between letters and placement of words), and make sure you have arrived at the most effective design before using the press-on letters. For heads that are based on a circular circumference, use a compass or perfectly round object to draw a base line in litho blue pencil and gauge the letter spacing carefully before executing the finished product. As the old poster on the office wall warns, "Think ahead."

When using wax letters rubbed from acetate onto the paste-up, a safer bet is to set the head on a separate strip of paper and then apply the entire head to the actual paste-up page. If, however, the staff prefers to press the letters directly onto the paste-up, and mistakes occur, they can be removed by placing a piece of cellophane tape over the letter in error and then peeling off. The adhesive will remove the wax. Care should be exercised not to tape over more than the spot in error, so as not to remove more than intended.

After setting headlines or borders with acetate or wax letters, be sure to cover the finished work with clean paper or the backing sheet from the letter sheet, and burnish well to insure permanent adherence to the page. Individual letters may easily be sloughed off in handling on the way to the print shop if care is not taken to secure them well. Some staffs prefer careful use of rubber cement for strips of type instead of the waxed backing provided by most print shops. Unless this wax adhesive is firmly burnished, even it may work loose enough for the type to slip or fall completely off. Double-stick tape on the under side of the top and bottom of type columns can help counteract this weakness. To avoid smudges and aid in keeping type placed correctly, the staff may find expenditure for clear spray or fixative warranted. It is also a good idea to cover each finished paste-up with clean newsprint or other paste-up sheets while en route to the shop to avoid slippages. Never place two finished paste-ups face to face, as friction may dislodge small elements.

When reversing type from a black or dark gray background, remember to allow at least one pica on all sides for framing. Use larger or boldface type to assist readability. And call for reverse type for only small amounts of copy. The reader's eye prefers black on white. Uniformly patterned screens are better backgrounds for type than ghosted photos with variations of tone. If ghosted photos are to be used and the background is variable, request that the photolithographer use the airbrush to even out the gradations.

One sure sign of a professional publication is the use of some typographical device to signify the conclusion of long articles, especially if jumping or continuing is a practice. Old-style newspapers insert a cut-off rule after the last line of each story. Cut-off rules are no longer used in this fashion, but many magazines employ small ciphers the same point size as the body type, which are placed on the last line, immediately after the period or flush right. Some are solid em squares (a square the size of the capital M), some are line boxes, some designs that represent the publication or its institution. These should be obvious, so that the reader need not wonder what the symbol represents. *Texas Magazine* uses a 9-pt. solid shape of the State of Texas. *Sports Illustrated* uses the word END; there should be no confusion over that. Typographical endings are not necessary, but they do add an extra touch to fine graphics in a publication.

Economy

Both time and money often can be saved by using preprinted material. Frequently student makeup artists become frustrated attempting to make straight borders from hairline tape. This is one spot where letterpress printing has it over offset for ease of operation; those metal rules do not waver so easily. It is a neat trick to use borders already printed in magazines or on ad sheets that might have been given to the yearbook staff. When you have found a printed box the proper thickness but it is too wide or too high, take a mat knife and make a diagonal cut at two opposite corners (top left and lower right). Trim away the printed portion (if any) inside the border and position the two right-angle pieces back together around the material you wish to box. Careful trimming at the mitered corners will produce a neat rectangle of any dimensions. These will look neater than a wavering tape line, and cost nothing.

Using preprinted material requires judgment. Never clip any copyrighted material such as comic strips or the faces of recognizable persons for use in your publication without permission of the artist or the individual, especially for use in advertising. You just might get sued. (Always get a model release when using photos of people in advertisements.) Preprinted material can be used, however, and most effectively in special designs. Travel folders can be clipped for pictures of famous landmarks. Sporting-goods catalogues provide drawings of equipment that might add a special touch to a headline or layout. And often just pieces of printed matter make good fill-ins or background pieces in a collage. Never reuse material from a newspaper; the paper is soft and fuzzy, the dot screen is too large, and the ink is likely unevenly distributed. Items printed on slick white stock resemble repro proofs such as one might get at an ad agency or in a publicity kit; they are screened and ready to paste down as line work. In using pictures printed in color, remember that your camera only makes tonal differentiations. Reds, purples, midnight blue, and black will all pick up dark. Pale blues and greens will fade together, and may fade all the way out. Choose printed pictures in which the contours are clearly defined by contrasting lights and darks rather than by faint tonal shadings. Pale gray spires against a baby blue sky will not make a clear image when reproduced in black and white.

Some staffs find acetate letters can run into too large a budget, so they attempt to reuse letters from "discarded" paste-ups (not old copies of newsprint images, original art pages for past issues). With the guide lines removed, it is a ticklish job to align these characters with the others in a word. It helps when a whole word can be reused, but on occasion a single letter is needed and the original sheet is out of that letter. Some staffers have been known to succeed in resetting the date line in 8-point type on the nameplate by cutting just the few numbers needed to bring Friday, April 19, 1974, up to Friday, April 18, 1975. First they cut a small hole in one sharp image of the old dateline (or the newly set line) for the 8 and one for the 5; then these figures were cut on pieces larger than the holes, from other nameplates, and slipped into the correct spots. Stick glue around the back of the replacement area or on the edges of the replacement numeral allowed enough slippage for correct placement. Rubber cement might ooze onto the image; transparent tape adheres once and leaves no margin for adjustment. All these pieces were taken from crisp letterpress reproductions on glossy enamel stock. The same benefits can be had from reuse of acetate type from original paste-ups, not from newsprint reproductions. Use of "magic" tape on the surface side to add or change letters may distort the image slightly under the camera's lights. Inserting from the back is the better choice.

Much expensive film-coated polyester overlay material has been ruined because of slips in attempts to remove the film coating. Cellophane tape is a handy tool for peeling away the film after the portion to be removed from the see-through backing has been outlined with the razor knife. A piece of tape picks up and peels away the film more cleanly than fingernails or the mat knife.

Get the most for your color dollar. When paying for a color run on any single page, remember that it costs the same to print a single period in red as for the whole page; you are paying for the plate and the press run, not the amount of ink used. Take advantage of the opportunity to include color on other pages that will be run at the same time. By printing some elements in 100 percent strength and screening other parts to 70, 50, 30, or even 10 percent of full strength, the effect of several colors can be achieved. Narrow borders and fine line work should get full-strength treatment; screens behind type or photos should be screened down to the lower tonal ranges. Do not attempt reverse body type over any but the darkest colors. Headings of large letters and few words most likely will stand up with lighter tones.

EXPERIMENTATION

Some tricks student photographers might want to try for special effects include use of fish-eye or wide-angle lenses. Their use is better for view scenes than for people pictures because of the distortion; but if the people's faces are not featured, there might be people in the photo for extension of the mood projected. A multi-image lens can produce a group of images on a single frame. Use of a small cardboard cylinder over the lens can be used to get several images on a single print with a standard lens. Shooting through a mesh screen produces rays of light or starbursts from light sources such as the sun through the trees. A few drops of water on the lens, or vaseline around the edge, will dramatize a picture. Of course, experimentation with use of filters can create some interesting distortions of tonal values. These tricks are to be used in "mood" photography, not journalistic documentary photography. Special films and screens produce specific patterns and tonal effects. Some "mistakes" that happen to beginning photographers have proved to be assets. One young man, hurrying to get football shots ready for the print shop, used developer that was too hot, and the prints came out with a pigskin grain. Luckily the staff viewed this pattern as an extension of the gridiron message, shaped the shot like a football and produced a most effective cover design. Had the pictures been of the homecoming queen, the false acne could hardly have been considered a desirable "effect." Photographers may sprinkle salt on the paper, expose through gauze, tissue, rice paper, or any surface that filters light. And, of course, the plastic screens with patterned effects can be used instead of paying the printer special-effect charges. Comparative costs and the probability of usage will influence the purchase of these items over paying the printer to supply them. Solarization of prints (exposing the paper to light before the print is exposed) can add to the kinetic feeling of rock music reviews. Time exposures of fast-moving action produce abstract pictures. If any subjects are stationary, such as microphone stands or buildings, they will emphasize the feeling of movement in the photograph. Or the camera operator can pan (follow the primary subject) with the lens to keep the main object in focus and let the background blur.

SUPPLIES AND EQUIPMENT

Some tools or materials that will add to the efficiency of the newsmagazine laboratory, not necessarily in order of importance, include:

> Lithographer's blue pencils for marking dummy sheets with instructions for the printer. (This blue will not be picked up by the camera in the plate-making process.)
> Erasers—art gum, kneaded, and soft rubber for various jobs in cleaning up paste-ups and art work.
> Liquid paper or opaque white to clean up smudges or scars on finished pages.
> Photo-retouching pigments with fine brushes for improving prints and other art.

Special Techniques and Equipment 143

Rulers—heavy metal with felt or cork backing for use in cutting clean straight edges; picas and inches or centimeters for measuring copy and layouts and cropping photos.

Artist's mat knives or razor-bladed knives with angular blades for cutting along straight lines and trimming, with swivel blade action for intricate contours.

Scissors with sharp, fine points, to trim curves or small contours the knife wielder misses, and to clip proofs and art for paste-up.

Paper cutter—the finer, the better, for photographs and other large sheets of paper. (It should not be treated as a toy by idle staffers with bits of cardboard.)

T square—accurate, for use in aligning material; several should be available. (Also not toys; should not be used for dueling or pseudo-sword fighting.)

Triangles—for use in aligning and positioning materials, not to be used as a cutting edge.

Smooth, square working surfaces—several, including light box, art boards, drawing tables. To be used for preparing dummies (not as carving boards or graffiti surfaces).

Paste-up sheets and dummy layouts showing exact page size, print area, column structure(s), bleed trim area, preferably scored with horizontal and vertical lines by picas or quarter-inches.

Sheets of hand-set rub-on letters of display type for use in special headlines. (A 30-pica plastic "headline setter," which comes with some brands, is a help for short lines.)

Smooth, round-tip burnisher for setting wax letters.

Smooth, flat burnisher for adhering film letters and waxed type to final layouts.

Border tapes, assorted widths and weights, both straight and pliable. (One that will round corners is called crepe tape; other brands offer rounded corner pieces for use with straight sections.)

Cropping L's, scanners, or proportion wheels for use in cropping and proportioning pictures. (Also not toys.)

Yellow grease pencils for marking cropping instructions on the face of the photo, or soft #1 drawing pencils for showing crop marks lightly on the back.

Red or black construction paper (better quality stock if available) or plastic red or amber material for masking windows on paste-ups where halftones are to appear.

Tracing paper or light-safe stripping film-on-polyester sheets (red or amber as above) for making overlays. These latter items are plastic sheets with opaque film coating that can be peeled away from areas to be clear. They are used overlay fashion, and the windows for halftones are left on the sheet while the rest of the page is peeled away to reveal the line art and type. They are especially useful for intricate designs of photo layouts, special area tint blocks (making only the apple red or the daisy yellow) on black and white compositions, and outlining photos for lightening or dropping out the background. Tracing paper is usually good enough for showing positions for small bits of type on overlays.

Rubber cement, stick glue, double-stick tape, transparent or cellophane tape, and, preferably, a small hand-held electric waxer to coat school-prepared type and art for paste-ups. The various adherents will prove favorites for different jobs for different people.

A cigar box or other sturdy container for rolls of border tape, burnishers, mat knives, etc.

Containers for all tools and materials, especially sheets of unused heading type, clean paste-up dummy sheets, used original paste-ups in case an emergency dictates reuse of some letters, and a safe box to store finished paste-ups waiting to make the trip to the printer. (Small bits of type or artwork can be dislodged and lost easily, borders can be crimped, and entire pages smeared, even wrinkled, if not cared for.)

A supply of magazines and other printed materials that might yield some needed piece of border or type.

The staff will find it prudent to keep all tools in their special storage places when not in use. It saves time searching for them and money replacing broken supplies, and it clears the working area for other jobs. Keeping the work area clean and free of extraneous matter will boost the efficiency of all efforts therein.

Appendix A

GLOSSARY

Air: white space around type to enhance readability.
Art: illustration(s), photographic or artist-drawn.
Ascender: portion of a letter that rises above the main body.
Baseline: imaginary line on which primary letters align at bottom.
Ben Day: shading patterns of various intensities used as borders or screens in line engraving or line lithography reproduction.
Billboard cover: front of a magazine containing type to call attention to several articles inside.
Bleed: extending picture beyond edge of page on one or more sides.
Body type: size and face of type used for the main part or text of printed matter.
Boldface: letters that are heavier and thicker without being higher than the standard type of its classification.
Box: typographical enclosure of type and/or pictorial matter; may be from hairline thickness up, solid black or shaded (as a Ben Day rule). Sometimes appearing only at top and bottom rather than all the way around—thus, a sideless box.
Budget: amount of editorial copy and art for an issue of a publication.
By-line: author's name appearing as part of the display with an article.
Caption: see Cutline.
Catchline: heading for cutline; appears between photo and cutline or to the side of cutline below photo; always larger type.
Cold type: type set by other than hot-metal process—may be photographically prepared, preprinted for rub-on use, or executed by strike-on machines similar to the typewriter.

Collage: art prepared by pasting together various elements into a single composition.

Column inch: unit of measurement used primarily for advertising sales; denotes one column wide by one inch deep. (Column width may vary with publications; standard column for advertising must be established.)

Comprehensive: exact-size, detailed dummy of a printing job, as nearly resembling the finished product as the artist can prepare.

Condensed: type that retains its height but has narrower characters.

Contact print: same-size photographic print made from negative without using enlarger.

Continuous tone: picture containing shades of gray between black and white, not screened to a dot pattern (a photographic print).

Contrast: a markedly different typographic or art element in a design introduced for interest or emphasis; definitions of light and dark tones in a photographic print.

Cover: to gather information and report on an event or a situation.

Crop: to eliminate portions of a picture that have no interest or conflict with the main emphasis; process of indicating by crop marks the portion of the picture to be used in reproduction.

Crop marks: indications in margin area of photographic print of the area to be reproduced, made preferably with grease pencil; may be indicated on back of print by drawing entire rectangle lightly with soft lead pencil by viewing through light box.

Cropper's L's: pair of L-shaped cardboard pieces that can be manipulated to find the most effective area in a picture.

Cut: metal engraving used in letterpress printing to reproduce illustrations; condense an article to shorten it.

Cutline: explanatory material that amplifies the message in a picture; tells that which photograph cannot (names, dates, etc.).

Cutoff rule: thin line of metal used between the end of one story and the headline of the next—an old newspaper device.

Density: quality of a photographic negative that controls passage of light and defines tonal gradations in the print.

Departmentalize: to group content of a publication by subject matter.

Descender: portion of a letter that extends below the main body.

Diagonal: geometric method of determining size of reproduction image of a picture.

Glossary

Display: type larger than body type, which is used to attract attention—headings, subheads, etc.

Dummy: preliminary layout showing position of text, illustrations, display type, and any typographical devices for a printed piece. Thumbnails are miniature and sketchy; roughs are full size but not exact in all details; comprehensives are exact in size and detail except that body text is indicated by perfect lines.

Duotone: photomechanical term for a two-color halftone reproduction from a one-color photograph, usually combines black and one color.

Extended: type that retains its height but has wider characters.

Flag: nameplate for a publication on front page; also logo.

Flush left (or *right*): type set to line up on an imaginary vertical line. (If aligning at both sides, copy is *flush*.)

Folio lines: lines giving name of publication and page number, sometimes date of issue.

Font: complete assortment of type characters for one size and face.

Format: physical characteristics, size, shape, style, typography, margins, etc., of a publication. (Full format usually refers to full-size newspaper page.)

Galley proof: long, narrow paper printed with newly set type to be checked for errors.

Glossy: photographic print on shiny-finish paper, preferred by printers for its ability to reflect light.

Graf: newspaper slang for paragraph.

Gravure: intaglio printing; image is incised into metal plate and ink from this transferred onto paper. Rotogravure is used to print some magazine sections for Sunday editions of newspapers.

Grippers: metal fingers on printing press that control flow of paper. Gripper edge of paper is the leading edge through press.

Gutter: inside margins where two pages of magazine meet at fold.

Hairline: thinnest rule used by printers.

Halftone: reproduction of continuous-tone artwork, such as a photograph, through a screen that converts the image into dots of various sizes to achieve light and dark areas.

Hand art: any artwork produced by hand as opposed to photographs.

Headline schedule: a collection of all headline types and sizes to be used by a publication; shows unit count and customary use.

Hot type: type cast in molten metal from forms in a machine or arranged in a carrying stick by hand.

Initial: first letter of a paragraph set in larger type for emphasis; used when headline does not ride over article opening, or in several selected spots through text for relief when subheads or story breakers are not used. Size is a matter of choice; some initials occupy a segment of the first three lines of text, others are aligned with only the top line and are called stick-up or rising initials. Use should be consistent.

Jump: to continue a story from one page to another.

Justify: in typesetting, to space lines uniformly to a set width; all lines fill column width.

Lead: (pronounced *led*) adding metal strips between lines of type to increase space vertically. Term is sometimes used for cold-type composition to "air out."

Letterpress: method of printing from raised type and metal engravings.

Line art: illustrations using only black and white areas as opposed to halftone dot patterns. Ben Day screens are considered line art.

Lithography: method of printing that transfers image from stone to paper; photolithography uses sensitized metal plate exposed photographically to create the image, which is offset to a rubber blanket, then to paper; hence: offset printing.

Logotype (or *logo*): distinctive design for the title of a publication, a section in a newspaper or magazine, or the name of a firm or advertiser; same as signature or sig cut.

Masthead: pertinent information concerning location and staff of a publication, mailing permits, memberships, and other public data; usually found on editorial page; may list advertising information.

Measure: length of line of type, or group of lines as in a column.

Mortise: area removed from a picture so that other material can be inserted.

Nameplate: same as flag or logo.

Newsprint: inexpensive paper usually used to print newspapers.

Offset: see Lithography.

Overlay: transparent sheet over a picture or layout to indicate placement of special-treatment elements or to separate portions of a printing job for individual treatment. Overlay must be marked to show exact position when the separate pieces are positioned on the finished piece.

Pica: unit of measurement in printing industry; one pica equals 12 points; size of characters for standard typewriter keyboard.

Plate: piece of metal that carries the image to be printed.

Point: smallest unit of printer's measurement; one point is $\frac{1}{72}$ of one inch.

Poster layout: typical tabloid cover page showing one photo or drawing and one or two headlines of stories inside.

Pyramid: placement of advertisements in newspaper graduating from wider at bottom to narrow at top; works against use of rectangular type blocks; incorrect for magazine pages.

Rectangular layout: page arrangement with content areas divided into rectangles that harmonize to enhance readability of the whole.

Register: positioning separate images or colors so that they match properly on printed page.

Reproduction proof: (*repro*) printed on white paper from perfect engraving or type ready for use in photomechanical process.

Scaling: reducing or enlarging illustration to scale for reproduction.

Slug: identifying line of type used by typesetter to identify a piece of copy; originally a "slug" of metal.

Spec: specification or instruction to printer on kind and size of type and line length for setting copy; any specifications for printing a piece.

Spread: two facing pages; center spread on the natural fold, or two single sheets that comprise facing pages.

Standing head: recurring heading for column or department, all or part of which does not change from issue to issue.

Stylebook: handbook for establishing consistency of style in grammar, punctuation, abbreviations, and the like.

Tabloid: publication format roughly half the size of full format newspapers, approximately 11 x 15 in.

Text: body copy set in type; "straight" matter.

Thumbnail: Miniature rough sketch of layout.

Tint block: various even tone areas (strengths) of a solid color, used behind type blocks or art to add emphasis; may be gray.

Unit count: measurement of number of units or characters for a headline that can be set in a specific type at a set measure.

Velox: a photographic print from the screened negative that was made for use in burning the printing plate in offset lithography.

Window: clear areas in page negative (line art and type in position) into which screened halftones will be positioned for plate-making; created on page paste-ups by placing dark red or black material in the exact space and of the exact size the photo will be.

Wrap: continue type from one column to the next; to set type at different measures to fit around an illustration.

APPENDIX B

BIBLIOGRAPHY

Books

Allnutt, Benjamin, ed. *Springboard to Journalism.* New York: Columbia Scholastic Press Advisers Association, 1973. Excellent condensed text for writing and designing for school publications.

Arnold, Edmund C. *The Student Journalist.* New York: New York University Press, 1968. Excellent basic text for scholastic journalists.

———. *Ink on Paper.* New York: Harper and Row, 1963. Solid handbook of graphic arts from the master teacher.

Craig, James. *Designing with Type.* New York: Watson-Guptill Publications, 1971. Excellent catalogue of tools of the trade, with workable tips on usage.

Dair, Carl. *Design with Type.* Toronto: University of Toronto Press, 1969. Still advanced in design presentation, classic examples, and exciting details of artistic approach to printed publications.

Hanson, Glenn. *How to Take the Fits Out of Copyfitting.* Fort Morgan, Colo.: Mul-T-Rul Co., 1967. Handy little guidebook for copyfitting; comes with measuring rule.

———. *The Now Look in the Yearbook.* Minneapolis: National Scholastic Press Association, 1971. Much of the approach to page layout is applicable to special pages in newsmagazines.

Nelson, Roy Paul. *Publication Design.* Wm. C. Brown Company Publishers, 1973. Philosophical approach to integrating formula and format, coordinating content with presentation visually and verbally; a very usable volume.

Pocket Pal. New York: International Paper Co., 1974. Graphic arts production handbook; explanatory, helpful reference paperback.

Strunk, William, Jr., and White, E. B. *The Elements of Style.* New York: Macmillan Paperbacks, 1962. Indispensable as the publication's own stylebook should be for proper language usage.

The Student Journalist Series. New York: Richards Rosen Press. A collection of volumes on various phases of scholastic journalism; especially applicable to newsmagazine staffs are those on writing by William G. Ward.

Turnbull, Arthur T., and Baird, Russell N. *The Graphics of Communication.* New York: Holt, Rinehart and Winston, Inc., 1968. A well-illustrated manual on the mechanics of printing production and the principles of graphic communication.

Ward, Bill. *Newspapering.* Minneapolis: National Scholastic Press Association, 1971. The best tips on writing from one of the better teachers of writing. Indispensable for content ideas and writing techniques.

Periodicals

Better Editing, American Business Press, Inc., New York, quarterly.

Columbia Scholastic Press Advisers Association Bulletin, Columbia University, New York, quarterly.

IABC Notebook, International Association of Business Communicators, Akron, Ohio, monthly.

Quill and Scroll, Quill and Scroll Society, University of Iowa, Iowa City, Iowa, bimonthly.

Scholastic Editor Graphics/Communications, National Scholastic Press Association, University of Minnesota, Minneapolis, Minnesota, monthly during school year.

School Press Review, Columbia Scholastic Press Association, monthly.

Taylor Talk, Taylor Publishing Co., Dallas, Texas, monthly.